AF578109

Dedication

I dedicate these memoirs to:

Baba Ramji;

Departed Noble Souls of

My Beloved Dad and Mom;

My adorable sons,

Anirudh and Navya who

have grown taller than me;

My sweet daughter-in-law, Ekta,

Who gave cute Naomika in my arms and

made me a Proud Dada;

and

all those who showered

their love on me.

I ALWAYS FLEW HIGH TO LAUGH LOUD

WHEN I FALL.. I STAND TALL

DR. ANOOP BHALLA, IFS

INDIA · SINGAPORE · MALAYSIA

Copyright © Dr. Anoop Bhalla 2024
All Rights Reserved.

ISBN 979-8-89186-387-3

This book has been published with all efforts taken to make the material error-free after the consent of the author. However, the author and the publisher do not assume and hereby disclaim any liability to any party for any loss, damage, or disruption caused by errors or omissions, whether such errors or omissions result from negligence, accident, or any other cause.

While every effort has been made to avoid any mistake or omission, this publication is being sold on the condition and understanding that neither the author nor the publishers or printers would be liable in any manner to any person by reason of any mistake or omission in this publication or for any action taken or omitted to be taken or advice rendered or accepted on the basis of this work. For any defect in printing or binding the publishers will be liable only to replace the defective copy by another copy of this work then available.

Contents

Preface

By the time I finished writing my first memoir "I wanted to grow chocolates in woods", I had superannuated from Civil Services.

Life was moving, but I can't say smoothly. I was more excited that since now with ample time at my disposal, I would just relax and enjoy my personal life. I would devote more time to my personal hobbies. My life partner and I started enjoying exotic vacations too. I started devoting more time towards my philanthropic activities.

Only 4 years passed; first, I lost my beloved father and by then, my beloved mother's dementia too had grown into Alzheimer's disease.

After I failed at growing chocolates in woods, I still didn't read Nature's message which outrightly rejected my wish.

As my habit goes, I love taking challenges. So, in the 2nd phase, I retook the same challenge. I thought that in this phase of post-retirement. The audience is new and private. So, the area required to grow chocolate too would be small. So, this would improve my chances of succeeding.

It looked to me – or was it an illusion – that my efforts were finally bearing fruit. The initial fruits looked to have a mix of sour and sweet taste but surprisingly, they turned bitter and dark! Even new fertiliser combinations didn't make any difference. With time, the odour of the crop too became so horrific that it became impossible for me to stay in the woods.

It reminds me of famous lines by Gulzar, "In life, before growing a plant of love, do test the soil first because every soil doesn't have an inherent nature of trust."

It now looks like my life has become like a court where every day, new cases keep on coming.

Somebody asked me the other day, " what's the cost of pain?" I replied, "No idea; because all gave me free." So, the fight to beat the second storm kicked off in 2022. It continues, but this time, it was not an ordinary storm. It was more like an earthquake. So, my inner thoughts started bothering me in the last year. These thoughts were shaking my soul day and night and literally forcing me to dig deeper to understand why my life has never remained calm.

Why does life keep giving me massive jolts the moment I have small happiness? Why only I am targeted by fate to suffer? Am I born only to bear miseries?

Reaching the age of mid-60s, why is there no end to turbulence in my married life?

I have been giving my best to nurture and groom the most pious relationship in Hindu Society with total honesty and devotion.

I had been only seeking love from my soulmates for leading a happy and fun-filled married life. But still, fate doesn't show any mercy in rejecting My WISHES for true Lady love continuously. Why am I being made to be humiliated and tortured by my spouses every time?

Not being able to bear more or say, I lost patience in fighting all along, I became so frustrated that I was left with no other choice but to find answers to my questions. So, to find answers, I planned to start my journey, however dark it may be!

My guts urged me, "Change is the biggest and settled law of this Universe" but "inner change" is the biggest challenge for humans. So, to bring inner change, you must accept this challenge of your own introspection. You have to deflower this life journey in a totally naked form.

Why this challenge became necessary was from two angles: one, that it's your duty as a citizen of this country to at least bring the harsh realities of our "liberal society" and their impact, especially on men, to the public domain. Second, the time factor, "Come what may, you must resolve this inner conflict which has been eating your brains so that you leave some real-life lessons for your kids to learn before you depart from Mother Earth!

Thus armed with a microscopic lens, I tried to bare my skin and expose my deepest thoughts with a vulnerability that even I was uncomfortable with. But I didn't stop to navigate the roads of my life from every possible angle. Especially, married life since it was this part of my life, I got "badly defeated". So that, at least, I know who was the real culprit. Whether it was Bhagya or Destiny or predestined or any X factor or myself who is responsible for what I got in this rugged journey so far.

I don't know whether, with my limited knowledge and skills, I succeeded in doing an honest introspection and located the devil or not... And what "change" or "transformation" it would bring in my life, in my persona in my remaining year? It is this introspection that I have tried to pen down as a sequel to my earlier memoirs...

PART 1

CHAPTER 1

It was on 12/7/22 around 10 AM, when I was informed by my servants that a disproportionate police force had come asking for me and demanding to open the locked main entrance gate of my residence, *DevSthali.* I was shocked but maintained my composure.

I opened my bedroom where I had been living like a prisoner since 6/6/22, locked my door and through the garden, reached my main entrance. I was surprised to see such a huge force headed by a lady SDO (police) and a TI.

SDO police just informed me that a complaint has been filed against me by my wife, but when asked to show the complaint, the team refused! While I started arguing with them, TI threatened me that if I didn't open the door, they would break the door.

My wife, on seeing the police force at the gate, started shouting at the top of her voice from the 1st-floor terrace, "This is my house. It belongs to my father-in-law. This man has been mentally and physically torturing me and has kept me here as a prisoner!"

I asked my servant to open the door and the police team called my wife, who quietly came down from the terrace. I hadn't seen her face since 6/6/22 and hated to see her face I unlocked my bedroom and relocked myself.

The police started their interrogation with her on the deck linked to my bedroom through a sliding glass door. I could easily hear their conversation as well as see what was going on the deck. I saw that they made her write her statement on the spot which the police force cleverly used it later as her complaint before visiting my house on 12/7/22.

It proved that before her recorded statement on 12/7/22 in my house, there was no complaint with the police.

I could see her younger brother, who stays in Indore, roaming in my garden and talking to the TI along and her local Uncle was sitting on the deck along with my wife and SDO(P).

After half an hour, I too was called by SDO (police) for questioning. Before going out, I sent a message to a lady police officer through my maid that I wouldn't come out unless my wife's brother and uncle were thrown out of the house. They left my house very reluctantly.

While talking to me, their tone, especially that of the TI, was quite arrogant. So, I told them that you should know how to talk to such a senior civil servant as well as a senior citizen of this country. When I asked her again for a copy of her complaint, the lady officer showed me the same statement that was recorded on the spot.

I told the SDO(P), "Why you are trying to befool me by showing her statement recorded here only half an hour back?" No reply was given.

She then started asking me some vague questions. So, I told her if you are keen on knowing facts, then record my statement. She said, "*Vo tou kar hi lenge!*" But neither asked me anything further nor recorded my statement. I went inside my bedroom again.

The police force just kept sitting on my deck, chatting with my wife who I could see was in a cheerful mood. It was evening when then took the statements of my three maids and it was around 5.40 PM when a message was sent to me by TI, "*Bhalla ko bolo, humare sath Thane chale.*"

I could understand that their further plan was to humiliate me more. So, I called up Gautam, a close friend of mine to talk to political bosses to stop all this nonsense.

Meanwhile, Police Constables along with SI started banging on my door and started shouting, "*Aram se Thane chale nhi tou utha ke le jayenge*!"

I replied from inside, "Why Thane? Whatever you want to ask, question me here only and I am not feeling well." But then, there was silence for the next 10 minutes and I saw the entire police force leaving my premises.

I got a call from Gautam that SP has been given a heavy dose but he told our man that he had direct orders from ADGP, Mr Rao, to harass Dr Bhalla and book him under section 498 of the DV Act!

That same night, she returned along with SDO (P) so I went out of my deck before the lady officer was about to leave. She asked me to open the door of the kitchen store.

I said, "You did your job brilliantly. Now, just leave so that I can do what I want to do!"

She left quietly and I too was about to go to my bedroom when Seema started, "*Apko hua kya hai aur maine kiya kya hai? Kitchen ka store kholiye!*"

Her audacity surprised me but I still calmly replied, "First you stabbed me in the back then you're asking now why I am bleeding…you shameless woman," and went straight to my bedroom.

That night on the bed, I just wasn't able to comprehend what had happened today. I just didn't realise that I was heavily bleeding!

The next morning, I started getting WhatsApp messages from my Raipur friends along with paper cutting of front-page news of *Hari Bhumi*, a local newspaper that FIR under section 498 of the DV Act and Sec 345 of IPC has been registered against me. The news item mentioned two bizarre things: one that "IFS *adhikari ke ghar se unki bandhak patni ko churaya gaya,*" and secondly, "*Adhikari Farar hai*!" By evening, this news had spread through various WA groups of IFS, Retd AIS, etc., across the country.

I just couldn't control my anger and felt like, '*I would've taken a bullet for her. Now, I want to pull the trigger.*'

Now, my biggest worry was to get Anticipatory Bail and avoid arrest because I had understood that with her setting with the police, they would surely try to arrest me. My hearing for bail was scheduled after 2 days and I spent the next 48 hours in hell.

But another shocker awaited me, when on 15/7/22 – the day of my hearing for bail – in the morning hours, my wife created a cheap and dirty drama.

It was around 10 a.m. when Seema forcibly opened my bedroom sliding window and started shouting and crying, "*Vo police wale aye hai apko lene par mai apko nhi jane dungi, aap unko ja ke bol do ki humara compromise ho gaya hai!*" She didn't allow me to close the window and kept repeating the same. "*Unse mil lo aur bol do na ki humara compromise ho gaya hai.*"

It took me a few seconds to realise what the hell was happening. I was told by my maids that the same TI along with 5 constables were standing outside. But the first thing I noticed was extreme happiness in her eyes, which was in total contrast to what she was saying. So, I told her standing next to her in my bedroom, "The twinkle in your eye is just a reflection from the blade of the knife with which you stabbed me in the back a few days back…"

While my wife wasn't stopping shouting at my open window; I called up my Advocate, Mr Choudhry, explained the scenario and then, put the phone on speaker.

He started firing my wife, "Police *ko apne kyu bulaya? Vo kis baat ke liye lene ayee hai aur kaunsa compromise? Humara koi compromise nhi hai, police ko jo bolna aap jakar boliye; Sir, kisi se nhi milenge.*"

After the phone call, I went to the window and told her, "I've had enough of your shit. So, listen to me very carefully. The knife you used to stab me in the back came in handy. I have used it to cut my ties with you… So, just fuck off!"

After that, the mysterious smile in her eyes went missing. She left the window and God knows what she told the policewalas but they left immediately.

After the police left, I got a call from my CA, who is also a family friend. He said that Bhabi had called him half an hour back and said that she would withdraw FIR but in exchange, I too should withdraw mine and my mother's Petition under the Senior Citizen Act as well as Petition in the High Court where we had prayed for her removal from DevSthali and to file FIR against her respectively based on my police complaints.

OMG! I just couldn't believe it, and after correlating it with the morning drama of the police, I just asked the Almighty, "I don't know what's worse: women who lie or women who think I am stupid enough to believe their lies!"

The same evening, I was informed by my advocate that the bail was granted in just 5 minutes of hearing with a remark by the lady judge that it was clearly a case of misuse of Sec 498 by the lady!

My first reaction to this news was a deep pain of betrayal and I knew that I had been stabbed in my back by a woman whom I gave a life in the last 7 years, which most of the women couldn't have dreamt of. What I gave to her wasn't a favour but it was my love and devotion to my wife damn it!

I was so 2 pissed off at that moment that if I would have it my way I would slit her throat with the knife she left in my back.

CHAPTER 2

I was just not able to focus on anything because I was feeling so humiliated since the image which I had built over these 42 years of service across the country was gone in just one day. In the eyes of the public, my wife had presented me as a "villain, woman exploiter" which was so traumatic that I even thought of taking my life!

What was killing me from inside was that I had been under the impression that both of us were quietly rowing our boat but never could gauge that she actually was drilling holes when I wasn't looking.

But for the next two days, I watched through my in-house cameras in the garden, on the terrace as well as recently installed cameras in the kitchen and drawing room while sitting in my locked room. I could see her fearless movements in the entire house, chatting and laughing on the phone without any shame as if it was a huge victory for her!

There was this new spark in her eyes. Seeing no remorse in her was a clear indication that she was attaching herself like cinder blocks tied to my ankles, and then inviting me for a swim in poisoned waters. She was staging this drama like oxygen. So, I needed to stay positive to take her breath away. I knew that there were many good seeds in me. So, I must avoid every bad soil in the world. My guts were forcing me not to allow such a negative and toxic lady to rent space in my head. Raise the rent and kick her out.

My mind wasn't stopping sending signals, '*Can't you see that she is like a weed? You must uproot her from your life before it spreads...she clearly is like a leech who would suck the life out of you...she is like a cancer that would spread until there's nothing left. She seems to be always hungry. She would eat you alive.*' She would pollute everything around me. I got a hunch that don't hesitate. Fumigate.

I was just not able to bear all this because she had intentionally violated my trust and inflicted a myriad of painful emotions. It's commonly said, "If a person gets involved with warfare, trying to defend or attack, then his action is not sacred. It is a mundane, dualistic, and battlefield situation." Yes, indeed my *DevSthali* had become a battle field and I wasn't sure when and how my wife would attack next.

As they say, "Letting go of toxic people in your life is a big step in loving yourself." Similarly, cutting people out of your life means coming to the realization that some people are a part of your history, but not a part of your destiny By now, my guts were calling shots. Darling, you are in charge of your life. You can do anything that you set your mind to. Get in the right frame of mind, set some goals and attack. Be proactive, take charge and remember that some of the greatest battles will be fought within the silent chambers of your on soul and you know that you are awesome.

So, I finally took a call to walk away from this toxic, negative, abusive, one-sided, dead-ended and low vibrational relationship because it probably might create more space in my life when I turn my excess baggage into garbage. Moreover, "Yesterday is not ours to recover, but tomorrow is ours to win or lose."

I wasn't prepared to defend my mother and myself against her female-centric domestic violence laws. Thus, I just couldn't think of any other option other than to run away.

So, I called up my younger son to reach Raipur at the earliest. I talked to a very close friend in Pune whose wife was running a renowned Old Age

Home named TAPAS and told him that I would be reaching there in the next 2-3 days to admit my ailing mother.

I also informed my elder son who was stationed in Pune about our visit. So, on 22/7/22, I literally ran away from my house in the morning in the car of my CA Pramod along with my mom. My younger son, who had reached Raipur the previous night, was waiting at the airport and we three boarded the flight to Pune.

While on the flight, my thoughts were, '*My wife and I were living together for seven years. I just couldn't digest that the person for whom I would take a bullet for is the one behind the trigger. So, I knew that this call of mine that sleeping alone is better than sharing my bed with someone who shares a bed with someone else when I am not around is the best call of my life.*'

We got Mom admitted on 22/7/22 in Tapas which was a highly specialized old age home only for Dementia/Alzheimer's patients and was also fully equipped with all kinds of neuro experts. Every day, all three of us used to visit Mom once a day for an hour or so. We used to take her for a stroll on the campus in a wheelchair. My sons would chat with her and she appeared very cheerful seeing her grandsons on her side after so many years. I was so happy to see her smiling after more than a month. While strolling, she would always hold the hands of her grandsons very tightly as if she never wanted them to go!

On the 3rd day, her permanent nurse informed us about Mom's "paranoid attack" last evening. In this attack, she kept shouting, "*Mujhe bacha lo voh mujhe mar dalegi!*" Although she used to have these similar attacks before her departure from home, I did lodge police complaints too against my wife. But I expected that with my wife no way near her, the attacks would subside.

I was highly disturbed. So, I talked to the team of Doctors of Tapas who said that she definitely is suffering from some shock but we have started medication for that.

The next few days again passed but the frequency of attacks started increasing and now she was speaking more in attacks like, "*Darwaje band kar do, vo aa rahi hai... seema mera gala ghont degi. voh mujhe mar dalegi.*"

I was getting tense over Mom's developments so I called up my neurologist in the US who had been treating Mom for the last 1 year and gave a brief of happenings in Tapas. After listening, he kept quiet for some time and then responded, "Uncle, God only knows what your wife has done to Aunty but it's clear that a fear has been embedded in her brain and the persistence of such factors could be lethal for Alzheimer's patients." All three of us couldn't sleep that night.

On 30th July, my younger son and I were getting ready to visit her when Tapas' owner Mrs Wankhede called me and informed me that "my mom is no more!" She'd had a massive cardiac arrest. My sons and I just couldn't believe it and we rushed. After seeing Mom's dead body, all three of us were in a state of shock. We all shouted, "Your knife, my back; my gun, your head." Anirudh added, "Papa, there are murders where the blood can be seen everywhere but there are also some murders where it's not the blood but only tears flow."

We three cremated her in Pune with full Hindu rites. Then on the 13th day, my younger son and I immersed her ashes in the Holy Ganga in Haridwar.

While returning from Haridwar, my younger son shouted in the car with tears in his eyes, "Papa, Seemaji should not have backstabbed. Her way to the top…sooner or later, karma is going to drop her ass."

I was in so much guilt that despite taking such a big decision to run away from home only to save my mother from the clutches of my wife, I still failed! First, social defamation because of my wife and just 20 days later, she snatched my mother. This all came so fast that sent my brain to nuts. I just didn't know how to move forward. I was getting into a deep depression.

One night, I just woke up from my sleep around 3 AM. Feeling restless, I went to the terrace, and unable to control my anger, shouted, "It's called karma. And it's pronounced *ha ha* fuck you. And fuck your sexual terrorism."

But I just wanted to find solitude. So, on 15th August 2022, after unfurling the Indian tricolour at my son's residence, I quietly left his house. I left my phone there and carried a small bag with whatever cash I had.

I took a bus for Rishikesh, and after a lot of running around, finally got shelter in a small Ashram called Shri Ramji Ashram on the banks of Holy Ganges in Munni Ki Reti.

The Ashram was headed by Baba Ramji, a saint who was quite heavy in size with a massive greyish-white beard, long white hair combed backwards and always used to wear a white dhoti wrapped from chest downwards. But he appeared to be a serious type of man, not speaking much. His face had *tej* and he had those speaking huge eyes.

On the very first day, after a cup of tea in the evening, I told him what I was going through and that I was there to be far away from the mad crowd to find solitude. His face showed no expression. He said, "In Hinduism, rivers are considered sacred and we worship rivers as divinities. They offer us an opportunity to worship God in his benevolent aspect. Maa Ganga has both pleasant and unpleasant forms. She is the creator as well as a destroyer and represents the very movement of life and the forward motion of time. She also exemplifies detachment, renunciation, duty, purity, sacrifice, and relationships."

I was really impressed not only with his knowledge but how with a resonating voice and in a simplistic way he presented his knowledge. Baba then said something which surprised me. He said, "*Prabhu Ram ne hi tumhari aatma ko aadesh diya isi liye tum yaha aye ho.*" Since I haven't been a spiritual man, his words just went over my head. I touched his feet and he blessed me, "Go to the temple to take the blessings of Prabhu and then, take rest."

The first 3-4 days were spent just sitting on the rocks on the banks and watching the Ganges flow just next to me. Since it was monsoons, the flow too was mighty and the sound of the flow was just mesmerising.

At night, while watching, the way Ganga was changing its course. Looking at the stars above, the guilt of Mom's death that had crept in staked out space in my consciousness and that caused plenty of emotional and physical turmoil.

Questions like, "Where did I go wrong? What more could I have done to save my mother? Why did I allow my wife to go near my mom which gave her the opportunity to torture her?" used to magnify my guilt to an unbearable degree. Every day, I was experiencing an uncontrollable anger that often used to escalate the moment my wife's face used to come to my mind. I used to cry at the top of my voice and shout, "Seema snatched my mom. Why you didn't stop it from happening? Punish her. Destroy her, Maa Gange." I used to weep like a baby sitting on the banks as well as in my hut for hours and hours.

But on spending more time watching Holy Ganga that was just moving on, varying its speed depending upon rapids, falls and hollows, I started comparing my life so far with the river.

There have been huge falls and some peaceful periods in my life too. And many a time, earlier too, I was stuck in life's hollow phases and now was passing through a similar phase. I have heard that life tests you. But in my case, tests were my whole life. So, I could hear Ganga shouting at me, "Son, you have to wait with faith and patience for the time and tide to change."

But unlike the river, I was resisting the way things had been happening to me in my life and this resistance was gradually persisting and becoming a burden on me. So, I could hear my inner voice saying, '*This is the best place to offload this burden.*' So, I decided that I would spend a minimum of 100 days here and see if Holy Ganges could give me solace as well as offload my resistance.

So, I came out of my shell and started spending time with Baba and the two workers of the Ashram, Radheji and Kailashji. I enquired from Kailashji about the age of Baba to which he replied, "More than 90." I was shocked because Baba didn't look more than 50. Radheji joined us and said, "Baba Ramji is very well-versed in the Vedas and other religious texts. He used to give long preaching talks to his disciples earlier but since last one year, he speaks quite less."

Gradually, I got back on my feet and started remaining busy in meditation in the early mornings and late nights sitting near the flowing Ganges, doing yoga and going for long walks along the banks of Ganges. I used to spend time in the dingy kitchen of the Ashram preparing dal, *sabji* and I learnt to prepare rotis too.

I was now happy, calm and at peace despite having no contact with the outside world. But I wasn't able to wipe off my negative thoughts like why again, after 18 years, I have been plunged into darkness by my 2nd life partner too? Is something wrong with me?

So, I started setting aside some quiet time daily for myself to prepare notes on my thoughts. I bought a few notebooks and writing pads from a nearby market and started penning them down. The more tried mentally to open the door to regret, writing down, the more and more emotions, anger and frustration used to surface, which was really pushing me to the walls!

So, while interacting with Baba one night after dinner, I posed my problem to him. He said, "Has Holy Ganga ever got frustrated after facing so many hurdles in its journey from high mountains until it's in front of you? How happy and mighty it looks. So, just calm down."

I said, "Baba! I won't sugarcoat this. In my experience so far, marriage, no doubt, is beautiful but quite hard. I had thought that it would be the most lively and romantic phase of my life but it turned out to be the one where a lot of compromise and sacrifice is needed from both ends. I kept on searching for that X factor but it kept on slipping out of my hands and I remained trapped in. It takes constant reinventing of myself to keep the relationship afloat. I tried my best to evolve with my partner and the relationship as well, since for me, marriage has always been commitment, sacrifice, consistency, and dedication. But it equally applied to my partner too. So, why did my partners not reciprocate? Both times, forgot about reciprocation; they back stabbed me and the present wife also virtually killed my mother. What do you make out of this journey, Baba?"

Baba quietly smiled and replied, "Our time on this earth is predestined. So, don't worry about your mother. As far as your other negative thoughts about failed marriages are concerned, tell me, how much faith do you have in God?"

I answered, "Baba! I have had faith in my karma only. Since the beginning, I have believed that by following the philosophy of 'work is worship', I am worshipping my God. And for me, work never meant just my job but all the responsibilities in all the roles being played by me so far in this life!"

Baba then said, "Good. Because that's one of the ways to please Prabhu. But have you ever wondered, what is the meaning of karma and how karma affects your life?"

It was getting interesting, So, I said, "For me, till now, Karma has had only one meaning. That is try to execute good and positive deeds in all my spheres of action."

Baba said, "Beta, karma is a concept in Hinduism and the common sayings, 'What goes around comes around' and 'What you sow is what you reap,' are great examples of how karma works. Karma also signifies the consequences of all the actions of a person in their current and previous lives and the chain of cause and effect in morality."

I smilingly said, "Baba, please just hold your bouncers...correct me if I am wrong but if God has created karma and karma means the activity associated with something...anything, it means that even God has to do something, correct? So, I am curious to know whether is karma superior to God. To give a little light to my statement, God can do anything, okay? But God has to do something. It means he has to think or do some kind of activity which is not understandable to the human mind. But if this thing is also considered karma, ultimately, is God too stuck with karma?

Baba smiled and said, "Being a science student, you think a lot but scientifically. Since you have no exposure to spirituality in Hinduism, you won't understand at this juncture. But you need to know that God runs this universe and controls us. So, don't question what He can do to prove His karma. But since you said that you are a believer of karma and since a particular karma runs on the principle of cause and effect, the result isn't determined only by the act but also by the intention. So, just tell me, did you have only these two ladies in your life so far?"

I said, "No."

"So, just try to think deeper, how had been your relationships with them? I don't think that Prabhu would have been so unkind there too. You must do this '*Manthan*' in your karmic journey to date."

Now this was something which I wasn't prepared for. Once back in my hut, Baba's words resonated. But since all of this was totally new to me, I wasn't able to understand what Baba was trying to convey to me. He was taking me into an area, which to me, was not only out of syllabus but about which I never cared or bothered.

So with pen and paper in my hand, I sat down on the sand and shouted at Holy Ganga, "From where to start and why to go back in past to analyse about all the ladies who came into my life; is it worth it? An inner voice shouted, '*Why the hell are you scared to look inside you? Did you do something wrong or committed some sin with those ladies?*'" My inner shouted, '*Never!*

I still remember that I was shaken. I wondered whether it was the Divine Ganga which talked to me just now. I felt internally so happy like, just when the caterpillar thought the world was ending, he turned into a butterfly.

Now, I felt confident that I needed to step back and rewind my journey to evaluate my karma, especially in my journey with the opposite gender since my adulthood.

I still can't forget that day in the ashram when I was getting ready to reflect back on that portion of my life.

Kailashaji came and said, "*Baba ne yaad kiya hai.*"

Excited, I literally ran towards his room. I saw a grown female elephant tied outside the main entrance of the ashram and a saint was sitting with Baba.

Baba told me, "*Tumne to kafi samay junglo me bitaya hai tou jao voh bechari bhookhi lagti hai?*" pointing towards the animal. Baba asked Radheji, "Atta hai?" He smiled, "Iske layak nhi hai."

I rushed to the market and brought 10 kg atta. Then, Radheji, Kailashaji and I prepared huge size heavy rotis. I learnt from the saint how to feed her and then, really enjoyed feeding her. She was so hungry that she ate all the 20-25 rotis we had made. I was very happy and pleased with myself.

The saint too was fed with food before he left.

He gave his blessings to me and said, "*Lord Ganesha ki tumhare par hamesha kirpa rahegi.*"

I had tears in my eyes which Baba was watching.

Back in my hut, I was so excited to start penning down my journey with all the women who came into my life.

PART 2

Rendezvous with the opposite gender

Chapter 3

When I started rewinding myself; it took me to my graduation days at Delhi University. I used to be a timid and shy lower middle-class school boy with almost negligible exposure to the opposite gender but still was very handsome. There came a sparkle in my eyes.

In the first two years, my target was to crack pre-medical and tried for 2 continuous years but couldn't.

Since besides my elder male cousin, my 2 other female cousins too had joined MBBS, the prestige of my parents went down, and due to this, I faced wrath from my parents. This broke me from the inside because it got deeply embedded in my little brain at that time that I was a failure and had let my parents down.

This pressure was so much that I just didn't enjoy my last year of graduation too. The only part I loved during my 3rd year in Hans Raj college days was *chaang* brew drinking in big dirty jugs with noodles or momos in the tents of Majnu ka Tilla with my Malaysian classmate Mutthu.

After joining PG in the department of Zoology, Delhi University's main campus, I was suddenly amidst a sea of female classmates. Many of them were quite beautiful and sexy. Now this was highly exciting for me. Many of my male classmates got busy picking up their female partners. Some did succeed in some kind of bonding or pairing. Some were trying and some were busy focussing on their studies.

I too was keen to have a girlfriend but my focus was to excel in my studies and prove my parents wrong. My physical features were changing fast making me more smart and handsome but still, no girl approached me. I too frankly lacked the guts to approach any girl.

Then one day, a 2-day excursion to Bharatpur Bird Sanctuary was announced. There, on the very first day, after settling down in a big hall of a Dharamsala, we all were trekking on the forest paths of the sanctuary. While our professor was exposing us to various birds, and their behaviour, I saw that one of my classmates, Geeta, started coming closer to me. She was quite beautiful and the best part was – I still can't forget – her curly hair, which I really liked.

We started talking and by lunch time, it became clear to me that she had been keeping a close eye on me in class and lab and thus, had developed a fondness for me. During lunch, she told me, "You are a simple but shy boy. You smile quite less, but when you do, it displays a true heart."

For the 1st time in my life, I heard these compliments from the opposite gender who had judged me in just over 2 months without even talking to me. I had no answers to her comments. So, I just kept quiet. When we were about to finish our lunch, she told me, "At least give me that killing smile of yours, Baba."

Anyway, by evening, we had come closer. She asked me to come for a walk. While walking on the kuccha roads of the sanctuary, she quietly held my hands. I didn't know but it was sure that both of us were enjoying each other's company. I could sense that. I am meant to be with her. I was getting a feeling of deja vu and this chance encounter was leaving me with an inner sense of recognition.

On the last day, a game of "Jam Session" was announced to be played by all of us at midnight in the complete darkness of our hall in Dharamshala.

I got a brief of the game from my classmates after dinner, and thus, I was so excited to play. Thus the moment the clock ticked 12 at midnight, like everyone else, I too rushed and started painting Geeta with toothpaste, shoe polish, jam, pickles, etc.

But Geeta just didn't digest this act of mine and got so infuriated that she literally threw me away. I tried my level best to explain to her that it was just a game. I apologised and literally begged her not to have any negative feelings towards me. But she didn't budge.

All my other classmates including girls too tried to convince her but she outrightly rejected their explanations.

I could see that the love and affection Geeta had towards me was thrown to the wind.

Back from the trip, I tried to meet her in the lab, library, and outside the tea shop but she kept avoiding me. Then, after 3 days, around lunch time, luckily with no one in the lab, I forced her to at least talk to me.

She point blank told me, "It's over!"

Thus, my first encounter with my 1st crush ended in less than a week, basically in one night. But why did it happen this way? What was my fault? What wrong Karma did I do? I couldn't find any answers. Why was Geeta brought into my life in the first place, only to be snatched the next day?

It wasn't easy for me to come out of this episode but decided to just move on. I completed my PG with flying colours but decided to try my luck in UPSC competitions. I really burnt mid night oil and finally, succeeded in getting into the illustrious All India Service, Indian Forest Service in the very first attempt. Getting into All India Services at such a young age of 22 years was an achievement.

After joining IGNFA, Dehradun in 1980, I gradually became more handsome and physically smart.

After 7 years of struggle since Graduation, I was finally enjoying my freedom in the Academy. I became popular amongst seniors as well as my batchmates. I was earning respect too, and this built self-confidence of my own worth.

I became part of booze parties at night and that too in all different kinds of sub groups from North, South, East and West India.

What I observed in those booze parties was that one of the agendas for discussion amongst my batchmates used to be their prospective marriage proposals coming almost daily from their parents.

I understood in a few months that being a Civil Servant was just like a goldmine. None of the officers used to have any guilt about it. In fact, they were highly egotistic about it. They cleverly used to cover it by ducking it as part of our culture and traditions.

But I don't know how but it was right inside me that marriage is the most pious relationship and not something to be preyed upon.

When asked how the hell your parents get these never-ending proposals, my batchmates used to say with pride, "Dear, our parents make efforts, give ads in newspapers, talk to marriage bureaus, pandits of the region, etc."

Since I was amongst the youngest officers in my batch, marriage wasn't my priority. But I definitely used to wonder why my parents never brought in the subject of my marriage during my holiday trips from the Academy.

After completing training in IGNFA, we went for the next short phase of our training in LBSSNA, Mussoorie. Here, there were trainee officers from the other two AISs namely IAS and IPS. There were many beautiful female officers from these 2 Services.

I used to remain busy playing lawn tennis, billiards, etc., so even the thought of locating any suitable girl for me didn't occur to me.

Just about a month to go before our departure from Mussoorie, I suddenly noticed one female IAS officer smiling at me from a far dining table while

I was collecting my dinner. I found out that Geetanjali was from Delhi and had been allotted UP cadre. She was beautiful, simple and cute.

A few days later, she met me in the lounge after dinner by chance. I was probably listening to some ghazal when she quietly sat in a sofa chair next to me. We exchanged smiles and started our initial conversation. Delhi was obviously the starting point but after spending a few minutes, I asked her to come for a walk on the campus.

During the walk, she started focusing on my hobbies and said that she was aware that I was a pretty good tennis player. After half an hour of walking, we came back to the lounge. She tried to be a little cosy and I did not object to it. Finally, after 15 minutes, we exchanged good night and left for our rooms.

Since our classes never used to be together, the only time we could meet was before lunch, evening snacks time or dinner. For the next few days, we somehow missed each other but one night, I reached quite late for dinner since I was boozing with a few IAS and IPS batchmates.

I was surprised to see her alone on one of the dining tables and she had probably finished her dinner. So, after filling my plate, I went to her table.

The first thing she uttered was, "It seems you aren't eager to meet me."

I told her that it's not like that. She told me that she had been to my room twice too but both times my roommate, an IAS officer from the South, had told her, "Look for him on the Tennis Courts."

I told her that this man just didn't inform me! I apologised to her and she sat with me until I finished my dinner. Again, we went for a walk but she was quiet. So, I tried to cheer her up with some jokes.

She asked me, "What are your plans?"

I said, "What plans?"

She said, "About the future."

I stupidly told her that since our training was coming to an end in 15 days, I was quite excited to join my cadre.

It was around 11 PM. So, I told her that since I have my lawn tennis finals tomorrow with P. Aiyer at 6 AM, we have to depart. I could see that she reluctantly agreed but held my right hand while walking back! The message was crystal clear.

But I, as a stupid man, still didn't take any initiative to meet her in the next few days. Then, I left for the Har Ki Dun trek for the next 4 days. After return, we met during evening snacks time and she enquired about my trek experience, etc. We decided to meet at dinner but missed out on my dinner again due to a booze party!

Then, I got busy with a few last exams but tried to look around for her on campus but she was just not to be seen. I enquired from her batchmates and was told that since the last few days, she hasn't been feeling well.

I still can't forget that day when all of us were loading ourselves onto the buses on the campus to finally depart from the academy and I suddenly noticed her standing at a distance.

I rushed to her and asked her, "Have you recovered?"

I could see that her eyes were moist but she didn't respond. She said, "Good luck with your career," and I reciprocated. She kept on staring at me as if she wanted me to say something. I was a big fool. I still didn't display guts or take that split-second decision to take her in my arms! We both shook hands and I left!

After we left Mussoorie, I as an idiot, didn't make any effort to contact her. God knows why at that moment I just didn't realise that I had done a blunder.

Thus, my 2nd encounter with the right woman who was clearly inclined to marry me too ended in a fiasco. She was the girl for me and now, when I reflect back, I feel she would have been my ideal life partner. But that wasn't written.

Now, this was two in a row. One at the age of 22 and the second at 25. Again, the same thoughts triggered, why did it happen that way? A God-sent opportunity was missed by me! Obviously today, I can say that it was bloody my fault. She was standing right in front of me with open arms but I, as an idiot, couldn't take her in my embrace.

I still recollect that losing Geetanjali remained in my mind for quite some time but I never gave time to ponder over why fate was snatching the right girls from me. What wrong was I doing that needed to be corrected? Today, I think probably, at that age, my mind set wasn't tuned to dig deeper and judge these events from any other angle other than just luck. Frankly, if I wanted, then even after reaching my cadre, I could have easily located Geetanjli but I just didn't even think about it. I feel that those were the mistakes I was committing but just didn't realise the cost I would have to bear later!

Although highly frustrated, I just moved on by diverting myself to the challenges awaiting me at the start of a new career. I also decided to go for an arranged marriage now and that too only after getting the 1st District Charge. That meant that I still had 2 more years to find a suitable girl for me. Good enough!

CHAPTER 4

So, once I joined the state, I got engrossed in building my career. Every day was a new challenge since knowledge accumulated in the Academy was of no use at all. It was a different ball game altogether. But I was not only enjoying the learning but was quite impressed, excited and thrilled with the status and power which would be mine in the next 2 years.

After spending a few months of my probation in the deep and dense forests, especially during my stays in Forest Rest Houses, my inner thoughts started surfacing. By that time, I hadn't been a follower of God but my inner guts started telling me that God is also nature, and thus, nature is God. Whatever you do in nature will have a resonance and finally, nature is the art of God. This laid the very foundation of my commitment to serve nature. A thought or a feeling got embedded in me right in the beginning that there was a purpose of God for getting me into the Indian Forest Service. I have been chosen by Him only to protect the water, woods, wild animals and the wilderness. I felt Blessed.

After being in the State on Compulsory Probation for a year by now, I became a target of my senior officers as an eligible bachelor. Suddenly, I realised that this "Punjabi Munda" was in great demand. Offers started pouring one after another from Punjabi as well as non-Punjabi Senior Officers, and all of them were quite high in the Cadre hierarchy.

So, I started getting invitations from the interested families and I used to be treated like a prince on such trips. A few of the matches were pretty good. I really liked one Punjabi girl and her family said "yes" immediately. Both of us spent 2 great evenings in Indore and she was all over me. She was modern in her thoughts and dress up, and had a PG in Humanities but had high regard for our Hindu traditions. Her father was a pretty senior IFS officer and was a well-respected figure in the Cadre.

But as an obedient son, I informed my parents about my selection and asked them to come over to meet the girl and her family. But I just couldn't believe it when they, sitting in Delhi, flatly rejected this selection by announcing not to go for any girl of your bosses since you would become a "*Ghar Jawai.*" Now, this bullet came from nowhere!

Gradually, I started getting scoldings from my bosses for this vague and immature behaviour of my parents, but I was helpless. At that time, I didn't show the guts to challenge my parents but my repeated queries of "Do you have any proposals with you?" to them used to be responded with, "What's the hurry? Have patience." A stage came in early 1984 when there was no proposal.

Today, may be not with conviction but still with the least doubts; I can say that if I had gone against my parents' wishes at that time and would have married that girl, I wouldn't have suffered in my career." My father-in-law was in such a high position in the cadre that I would have had the best of postings and a God Father to save me from all vagaries of a corrupt administrative environment. But that wasn't to be!

So, now there were three encounters in a row with the suitable girl right in front of me. But still, all of them slipped out of my hands! So, was it the fate or some force which was checkmating me on a regular basis?

My time for Independent District Charge was only a few months away but I had no clue about my marriage and future. At this juncture, my mom, out of the blue, gave me a proposal suggested by our neighbours in Delhi. She told me that they had seen the girl and she was pretty good.

I asked Mom if they enquired about the girl from her own sources and if they had shown the girl's *patri* to a good pandit.

My mom replied, "No need to verify the girl's credentials since our neighbour is taking full guarantee and I don't believe in patris. But the other side has got the patris checked and they matched."

I met this girl Neeru and rejected her outrightly. But as time passed, again there were no more proposals coming from my parents. Now comes the real twist. So, in my utter desperation one late evening, I called up my parents and told them that I had changed my decision and that we should go ahead with Neeru. I was so frustrated that I told them, "Go right now and communicate our decision."

That's how my 4th encounter was converted into getting my life partner finally. If I look back, I can easily see that some unknown force created such circumstances or situations for me to make such a split-second decision. It's quite intriguing to see how my 2nd and 3rd rendezvous girls who were the right girls for me were just teasers to make fun of me. Was this all pre-planned? Was it a conspiracy to bring in Neeru, who I had rejected and was brought into my life from nowhere? I still can't figure out this game. Who was playing it? Why was He playing it? Was it for my good future? I don't think so.

Neeru's entry into my life was the biggest turning point of my life! Her contribution to my life was only to make me a father to 2 cute sons but otherwise, I couldn't have dreamt of what she sucked out of me.

What happened in my marriage with Neeru has already been described in detail in my 1st Memoirs, "*I wanted to grow Chocolates in the Woods*". So, there's no need to rehash the details.

But again, this proves that Neeru was forcibly introduced into my life only to ruin my married life. Was she sent only to acquaint an innocent and dedicated husband with new words like deceit, cheating and backstabbing? If so, why? What wrong Karma did I commit which turned my life upside down? Why I was made the target by fate? Why I was being treated so unfairly?

PART 3

Restoration to intense misery

CHAPTER 5

By the time my first marriage ended in a disaster, I had crossed the age of 50. With no partner and most importantly with my kids too deserting me, my life was like being in a desert.

But I remembered, '*When life shuts a door, open it again. It's a door. That's how they work.*'

So, I decided to move on and open the doors. I also took a conscious call that until now, I had lived only for others, but now, I would live for myself. Why should I suffer in terms of a companion too? I trusted my guts that I deserved better treatment and had the right to make an effort to find my new life partner.

Although I was so disgusted with my break up that I started concluding that all women are alike in this Kalyug. And thus, had lost faith in the women. But another view too was circulating in my mind. It was that our Hindu society still has women of strong and dedicated character. Mine was sheer bad luck and probably, there was no dearth of good female souls."

Many would question this call of mine. There is a famous saying, "If at first you don't succeed, then skydiving definitely isn't for you." But since I had actually skydived twice in real life from 11,000 and 14,000 feet, I wasn't scared to jump again!

But yes, this was my call. My thoughts at that stage were that in my marital relationship, by now, I had remained ideal and sober and was a giver. It's only because of this attitude of mine that I have been taken for granted and even exploited. But now, since an opportunity has come into my life, I need to fine-tune my approach to have a new partner but live for myself and fulfil my personal wishes too. I didn't care how the society would perceive my decision. At that time, I didn't even care whether I would fail or succeed.

Since I was ready to skydive again, I enrolled myself on 2 matrimonial sites just to assess whether a person of my age had any takers or not.

I was shocked when the offers started pouring in within a few days. They were from a cross-section of women, unmarried, divorcees, widows, and more importantly, much younger than me. I finally closed down to 4 of them and took time out to meet them in Delhi, Bangalore and Chandigarh. I was highly excited about this phase. In 3 cases, intimacies were built in a short period of time since I could judge their honesty. All the 3 ladies were beautiful and caring and I was surprised that all 3 gradually started falling in love with me.

My parents were fully aware of what I was doing. They used to pass judgements about each of them but I hardly paid heed to them. But I used to tell my mom that since you had all the time pretending to be worried about my life, telling all our relatives so, I am not stopping you from making efforts at your end too.

This was the time in my life which brought back memories of my first 3 encounters. I could see women falling in love with me and loving every bit of me even at this age. Mind you, this wasn't physical at all and I could see it and feel it coming straight from their hearts! I admit that I got physical with all three consensually.

After spending a few more good times with one including a short vacation in Goa, I closed my hunt to Sarabjeet who was a Sikh, 10 years younger and unmarried till date. Both of us had fallen head over heels madly in love with each other.

The time I used to spend with her used to make me feel like I had already met and known her before. With her, I could relax and breathe easily. I was free from any anxiety. She too always allowed me to enter her personal space. My mind was calm as I felt comfortable around her. She was just a free bird, and despite a lot of family issues, she always had a carefree approach.

Sometimes, you meet someone and it's so clear that the two of you, on some level, belong together as lovers or as friends.

You meet these people out of nowhere under the strangest circumstances, and they help you feel alive. I don't know if that made me believe in coincidence, fate or sheer blind luck, but she definitely made me believe in something.

When I was with her, I had this gut feeling that she was *the* girl for me. So, after a few months of courtship, I took the leap of faith as I knew what was best for me and proposed to her.

She said with tears, "I am blessed to have a man like you."

Straight after proposing to her, I returned home excited and opened the subject of my selection for my 2nd life partner, this unmarried Sikh girl (whom they knew). I got such massive firing from both Mom and Dad that I just had no clue as to what they were saying! In the next half an hour, both banged me left and right with their flurry of accusations against her that I was dumbfounded. I only asked them, "Have you met her or any of her relatives?"

They roared and said, "It's our long experience and we can easily see through a girl."

Now, this was going haywire and thus, I just couldn't take it anymore. So, I quietly told them, "I am 51 years old and have more than desired wisdom to make decisions about my life. I am not going to repeat the mistakes which I made in choosing my 1st partner. Thus, I am going ahead with this girl."

To this, both of them retorted, "Fine, leave this house and our relations are over." Now, I never expected this kind of bargain to come from my parents.

But finally, as a fool once again, I accepted and honoured their decision.

A poor lady who loved me from the core of her heart and had all the ingredients to become my "soulmate" was left by me. All the dreams which we both had seen about our bright future – even had dreamt of a baby... she wanted to have a girl – got buried so fast. All my efforts and *paryatan* over the last 2 years went down the drain. I had come so close to achieving happiness after almost 7 years but still...

Now, the bigger task ahead of me was communicating my decision to my "soulmate." I was filled with so much guilt that I had no guts to face her. In fact, I was ashamed to even talk to her.

Finally, I decided to meet her. When I disclosed everything, she started crying like a baby after putting her head on my lap in my car. After a few minutes, she gathered herself, and in a sober tone, started saying, "You, at this age of 54, are still a stooge of your parents. We both are fully aware of how they have been trying to chain you for long. But you better be ready to face more wrath from them and suffer more. I still would remain with you as a true friend because not only I have loved you but I also know that you would need me in times to come."

I was just not able to recover from the shock of losing my chosen partner. This was the year 2011. I again was getting scared that if once again Sarabjeet was a teaser and fate has again planned entry of someone else? I was getting irritated and frustrated and this frame of mind started reflecting in the meetings. This mindset started affecting my image. With 6 years to go for my superannuation, I was also at the most crucial phase of my career and since my last promotion was at my doorstep, I didn't want to lose that. I had made big plans on how to lead the State with all my innovative plans.

But once again fate took a turn and out of the blue, one of my close friends, Jaideep, in Raipur asked me to have a look at a divorcee girl, Seema from Bhopal. Seema's 1st cousin was working as a petty manager for my friend and I had met him a few times.

Seema was 15 years younger than me and had been single for almost 7-8 years after her mutual divorce one year after her marriage. I met her at my place but based on my instincts, rejected her outrightly. But she didn't lose hope and kept on pressing my friend, Jaideep. After a month or so, based only on his positive feedback, I thought of reconsidering. My focus was on her very short marriage, her age, her family background and her independent financial status. I just didn't bother to verify her past. I didn't analyse why a girl with only 1 year of marriage hadn't been remarried for so many years. Why was a lady so desperate to enter a live-in relationship with a partner 15 years older than her?

I still can't forget in hindsight that two of my close friends, who were big-time Astrologers, had advised me not to go for this girl after matching our horoscopes, especially due to her weak character. But still, I didn't listen to them. I even didn't bother to wait, try to spend more time with her to know her more and understand whether she had the ingredients to become my life partner! But God knows how I concluded that she has the potential of becoming a caring partner. Obviously, it was my call. Why did my instincts not warn me? Why did my guts allow me to give her the benefit of the doubt?

My parents once again were furious over my decision but this time, I stood to my ground. Today, I feel that this time they were right. But I went ahead because this time, my younger sister and brother-in-law were there to give their judgment in Seema's favour. Before giving consent for Seema, we made it very clear to her as well as her family that live-in starts but until my retirement, she would visit me only once in 2-3 months and that too for a maximum of 2-3 days only. There would be no formal ceremony, and also at this age, I wouldn't allow her to demand a child from me. I had also clearly informed them of the current status of my divorce and committed that I was trying my best to get it.

But still agreeing on my pending divorce as well as my conditions, she and her family agreed to start live in relationship immediately. In hindsight, I do wonder now that at that time being a cultured family, if they wanted, they could have waited or could have refused to start live-in. Why did they accept my promise of obtaining a divorce from my 1st wife at the earliest? But it seemed that they were in fact in a hurry to start live-in ASAP.

This is how our relationship started in 2011, but since I was still in service, I tried to keep it very low-key and secretive so that people don't get to know about it.

Her visits to Raipur started once in 2 or 3 months but only for 2 or 3 days. She herself used to plan these trips mostly on weekends plus on state-declared holidays. She had no inhibitions to get physical with me from day one.

Anyway, I was finally happy but life said, "LOL, wait a sec." There was a clear understanding that there would be no formal ceremony, but still, after 2-3 trips, she started luring me to have a small formal ceremony! I didn't agree to such a proposal because it was clearly a breach of her commitment.

Finally, in one of her trips to Raipur, there was a heated exchange between both of us for this ceremony and I could clearly read that taking advantage of my status, there was indirectly an open threat. I had no option but to agree to it and the date of that ceremony too was selected by her as 11/11/2011. It was a ring exchange ceremony at my residence.

After this ceremony, in the next 2 or 3 of her visits, I started feeling that she wasn't a lady whose priority was me but most of the time, her focus used to be her family in Bhopal. Except for my sister, she wasn't keen to build relations with my other family members.

Another thing which I noticed was that she was habitual of changing her statements every now and then. Whether it was related to her past vis a vis her 1st marriage or about her job or about her family members; she would give different versions every time. This was something which used to raise red flags but I ignored it initially.

I also was watching that being habitual of lying, she either wouldn't respond when you would seek any clarifications of her acts or would play with only a few chosen words to completely deny my observations. My communications were always naked facts but they would be thrown out of the window as if I had fabricated them.

I used to wonder whether my selection of her as my partner by only presuming that belonging to a 'cultured family' she would be caring, loving and respectful to me and my family was right.

But then I started asking myself whether I was making the mistake of unfairly expecting her like to be more like the way I want her to be. Not at all! Because of my experience, I knew that sticking around in the hopes that someone would change for the better would likely only lead to disappointment.

Moreover, honesty in my marital relationship has always been my top priority. I always wanted to trust my partners completely but also expected the trust to be reciprocated. I cannot bear to be kept in the dark over any matter by my partner. I have always preferred to know the truth, regardless of how unpleasant it might be.

Thus I waited for her next 2 trips. I saw no change and also saw that she was taking these trips purely as a vacation to just enjoy and have fun. I noticed shockingly that she had no inhibitions about drinking. A girl who looked simple at face value was showing her real colours.

I started thinking, "*Life was much easier when apple and blackberry were just fruits.*' But I took a conscious call that this time, I wouldn't allow things to go out of my hands and suffer. So, without wasting any time, I said to myself, "*I'm ready for some warm weather. Spring has fooled me,*' and ended the relationship in early 2013 (virtually only after 1 year).

Today, when I look back, I think I made the right and logical decision.

By now, I just didn't realise how the last 8 days had passed. Since Baba was away to his other Ashram up the hills, I had all the time to spend on my daily rituals and completing my introspection. But I was quite eager to meet Baba now and brief him about what he had asked me to do.

CHAPTER 6

After 2 days, I was told by Radheji, “Baba is back this morning and was enquiring about you.”

I changed myself to my regular kurta pyjamas and went straight to Baba’s hut. He was sitting in his temple and gestured to me to join him. After 20 minutes of the puja, he got up and had his usual glass of milk. Then with a smile, he asked me, “*Manthan ho gaya pura*?”

I replied, “Yes, Baba, almost.”

Baba responded, “*Fir kya samajh aaya*? *Kya 2 kiya tumne aur un istariyon ne tumhare sath*?” I said, “Baba, the biggest mystery after this introspection is why the right women were brought into my life but snatched only to bring the wrong women into my life.”

Baba started laughing and kept on for some time. Then, he asked me, “What does your scientific brain say about it?”

I replied, “It only says that you were at fault. You were an emotional fool and you lacked the wisdom to take the right calls at the right time.

Baba said, “You need exposure to spirituality to find answers and for that, you would have to understand the role of God in shaping our lives.”

Baba then asked me to narrate the story of the period from my break with Seema till now. I told Baba, “It’s quite boring, so let’s forget about it.”

He said, "*Bahut notes bana liye ab khul ke sunao.*"

I said, "Ok, Baba, if you insist..."

After the break-up, to my surprise, Seema kept on pressuring me to take her back. She kept on sending emails saying, "I need you," "I won't disappoint you," etc. But I remained adamant and kept refusing since she had lost my trust.

But I couldn't digest why she didn't want to lose me. Where were her and her family's self-respect? At that time, I could only guess that may be because of the life she saw in those 5-6 short trips to Raipur, she and her family had their eyes on the luxurious life in the future and just didn't want to lose that.

But she still didn't lose hope and kept chasing me and my sister for 3 long years. It was in the year 2016 when her family requested a meeting. My parents were already with me and my sister and brother-in-law too flew in. In the meeting, she and her family members indulged in all kinds of dramatics of apologising on behalf of Seema's behaviour. They made commitments that she wouldn't repeat her mistakes and begged us to take her back.

To counter their verbal commitments, I told them, "Firstly, I have zero trust in their statements and secondly my 1st wife has flatly refused to give divorce. In this scenario, it's just not possible for me to restart the live-in despite your commitments."

Despite now knowing fully well that there would be no divorce of mine from my 1st wife and thus their daughter's legal future is dark, I was expecting that they would withdraw their demand to take her back. But to my surprise, still, her family focus remained pressing us and emotionally blackmailing us to take her back. Why? It still didn't raise any red flags at that time.

On the other side, I observed that my brother-in-law and sister were getting carried away by their family's emotional acts and were trusting their promises. So, we excluding my parents went to another room where both tried to persuade me to take her back. God only knows what made me accept their advice. I remember my father warned us, "You people are making a big mistake. You would repent because this girl is very cunning. I can see it in her eyes. She is a big actress and in the future, her family will swallow all your assets." But since my brother-in-law and sister were pushing the agenda in her favour, it was finally decided to go ahead.

This decision, I won't forget, because probably it was the only decision of my life which I made on the advice of other people.

Although live-in restarted in 2016, it was in stressful conditions since due to a conspiracy hatched, my due final promotion was snatched by the State. This was the biggest setback to my career and I had fought tooth and nail to get what I deserved.

But not bothered by what I was going through, Seema was back in her original colour after two trips from Bhopal. She started showing her keenness to shift permanently to Raipur, which I kept refusing. I told her to have patience for one more year and if anybody got to know of our cohabitation despite my first wife being alive, whatever was left of my career now too would be doomed.

But after a month, she landed with two huge suitcases and declared, "I have brought all my clothes. No more visits from Bhopal and thus, I don't care how you manage it." I was left with no option but to accept her "dictate."

But almost every month, there used to be fights on observing that she still continued to be careless towards the house and me. She would never show through her words and actions that the relationship meant a lot to her. She would rarely open the doors of communication and express her thoughts and emotions clearly about what she was really thinking. Most of the time, her conversations would revolve around her family members, their activities, etc.

I wanted to grow in the relationship and wanted her to become a mature and dependable partner. For me, physical intimacy and touch have always been significant in a marital relationship. It was my way of feeling connected to my partner on a deeper level. But for me, the physical connection never meant sex all the time. It could be something as simple as a hug, holding hands or a deep kiss.

Like she always wanted a bit of pampering from me, I too loved to be pampered equally through romantic and love gestures. I too wanted to be through simple caring gestures which, in my opinion, go a long way in cementing a relationship into an unbreakable bond. After a long and tiring day in office, I always wanted to be greeted with a smile and a warm hug. But all of this was missing from my married life. I used to wonder why a young lady who got divorced within a year and couldn't get remarried for almost 10 years still didn't want to behave like a newly married woman and express her love towards me. The answer I got was, "Damn it. She is on an entirely different flight path."

I could see that after my retirement on 30/7/2017 and shifting to my new residence, DevSthali, she started becoming aggressive in her demands for granting legality to live-in. I also observed that she always tried to be least communicative with me whereas I used to display my keenness to spend quality time with her.

I stopped my narration and asked Baba, "*Agar bor ho rahe hai to band kar deta hu?*"

Baba replied, "*Kisi ki aap beeti ko pehli baar sun raha hu aur dekh raha hi ki iss kalyug me prani kis tarah se nibah rahe hai aur tum jaise sache insano par iska kya asar padta hoga, yahi soch ke Mann thoda dukhi ho raha hai par yeh batao ki tum iss kalyug me kaunse satyug ke asulo par chal rahe the?*"

I regained my composure and continued with my narration...

Right from my 1st marriage, I had maintained this theology that to communicate clearly and consistently with your spouse is an essential tool for developing a healthy relationship. But the 2nd time too, I was finding myself in a situation where clear and reassuring communication was insufficient. I started feeling confused and lonely and left with mixed signals because I didn't know how and what she was feeling.

For me, it was important to realize that I am still the one in control of our relationship's destiny going forward. My priority had always been to have a partner who has the qualities that are actually important in a relationship, such as shared morals, values, and life goals.

However, her lack of productive communication started taking a toll on my mental health over time. I started feeling anxious, insecure, and lonely with feelings of uncertainty as to where I stood.

So, I started forcing her to sit with me and be honest about her feelings since it is the heart of good communication. In one of such sittings, I told her, "A husband is like a fine wine; he gets better with age." The next day, she locked me in the cellar. I was watching that instead of being truthful with each other, she started sweeping my feelings under the rug.

So, I used to wonder what could be the reasons. I started thinking that probably, she didn't have enough empathy for me. But it's so easy to get caught up in what we feel and need and worry about that we forget to take into account what our partner is feeling. It may not be a character flaw – it's just part of being human. So, I tried to put myself in her shoes and imagine what she might be thinking, feeling, and going through. I was desperate that since the stakes were high, I didn't want a situation to arise when the consequences could be devastating and by the time I realised that it was a communication issue, it would be too late.

Giving her the benefit of the doubt that she isn't my competitor and I am not in it to win it, I started thinking, '*Maybe, she doesn't always know what I feel or what I want. And maybe because for some reason she just can't put as much focus into the relationship as I like. Life gets in the way from time to time. Was I making her responsible for keeping me happy? Could this be the reason why my communications are becoming clouded by frustration and the weight of all those expectations?'*

On one side, I was making such hard efforts to build a healthy and transparent relationship. But at the same time, she was only interested in shopping, wanted lots and lots of jewellery and trips within and outside the country. Her drinking was becoming heavy and her interest in Bhopal too was increasing.

Most importantly, despite being in a live-in relationship, I, from day one, was giving her the status of being " my wife" and not a "live-in partner" amongst all my relatives, friends and colleagues. I gave her full freedom to move around town, visits to Bhopal were allowed, money flow to her through cash, new bank accounts, and credit/debit cards was more than desired. She neither had any money nor any jewellery of her own since 2011, but now, she had money in banks and jewellery, which any Hindu Lady would be proud of.

She thus was getting not only the social stature of a "wife" but was also getting a luxurious life which she wouldn't have ever dreamt of. But all through, my gut feelings were saying, '*Hey, watch out. Something is missing. Try to read.*' But like a fool, I ignored those inner calls and with sheer honesty, continued giving all the love, care and emotions a Hindu wife deserves. All with the hope that she would at least become caring towards me.

I was such an emotional fool that only to satisfy her constant demands during this period for granting legality to our relationship; in the year 2018, I got my Will registered with all my immovable and movable assets in her name and nothing for my 1st wife and sons. When I showed her the Registered Will, she just kept quiet but then said, "I am not interested in your money. If you want to give all to your sons, I have no objection."

All of a sudden in 2019, she started prompting me and my sister to hold a marriage ceremony with Hindu rituals. I straight away refused it by saying, "I can't do it since my 1st wife is still alive and she could charge me with bigamy."

But she kept the discussions alive and now started pressing me, my sister and my brother-in-law. By now, she had taken both of them in her good books. So, after some time, my brother-in-law advised me to have that ceremony. It was held at my residence where members from both families were present.

Despite a clear understanding that there would be no pictures taken of the ceremony, her family members secretly took pics as well as videos. This was shown to me by her roughly a week later. We had a big fight and I told her, "You should embrace your mistakes." But she hugged me.

It was getting clear that she had started taking me for granted while I wanted to feel valued and appreciated and be a priority for her. Also, on a daily basis, I was displaying acts to prove that I value her. With her being my wife, I desired her to become a complete partner. I never wanted her to remain only my wife but a true friend, in front of whom I could let my guard down and confide. But she still remained totally inconsiderate towards my needs and thus, the degree of harm to our relationship was escalating. I used to ask myself, '*Whether marriage is a workshop, where the husband works and the wife shops?*'

In this period, my communication with my younger son reopened after a gap of 16 long years. I went to meet him in Delhi just for a day. He introduced me to his fiancée, Ekta, who was working at the Bank of Scotland in Gurgaon and told me that both were ready to get married. After chatting with her in the car, I found that she was a good match for my son. So, I told him that I approved this match and asked him, "But what's the hitch?"

So, he said, "It looks awkward since Bhai (my elder son) is still unmarried."

I said, "So what? Since Ekta's parents are pressurising for an early marriage, just go ahead."

Acting on my advice, my 1st wife took a call, and within a month, the engagement was announced. I booked my air tickets and also a room in the same hotel in Delhi where the ceremony was proposed.

I don't know why this thought came to my mind to use this occasion for a bargain. Before throwing the bargain, I had discussed it with Seema and she neither opposed it nor was happy. So, I asked my son, "I would attend the ceremony only if your Mom agrees to give me a divorce." I was informed by my son after 2 days, "As a collective call of the family (including my elder son) we reject the offer."

After this rejection, I cancelled my trip to Delhi but the damage became bigger when I wasn't even informed of my son's marriage 6 months later! Again, the status of my relation with my sons was back to square 1. In hindsight, when I look at this Act, I know that it was the most stupid of me to play this sort of game with my own family and that too at a time when there was a reunion with my own family after 16 years. But frankly speaking, this idiotic thought of striking a bargain was again to satisfy Seema.

So, I decided to change my flight path…not to think that deeply and enjoy my life as an individual. So, more and more luxurious vacations within and outside India were organised by me. Some trips were as a couple, a few with my sis and brother-in-law and a few with a group of my selected Batchmates. I started having a booze party on my deck almost every night. Since both of us were good singers, we used to have real fun on these nights with karaoke. She was very happy with this change. This attitude made me calm and relaxed, rejuvenated me and brought back my energy levels.

I also adopted a new approach that it is better to remain silent and be thought a fool than to speak out and remove all doubts and started enjoying my life with the motto, "It's my life. I would enjoy it the way I want."

But after a year, she suddenly told me that her brothers wanted to get our marriage registered in Arya Samaj and they would manage everything.

I was so fed up with these stupid demands that I didn't object at all and they got a "fake marriage certificate" from Arya Samaj.

At this stage, Baba suddenly shouted, "*Tumhari ankhe band thi kyaa? Tumhe Prabhu Ishare de rahe the par tum kaunsi duniya me jee rahe the?*"

I hadn't seen Baba losing his temper like this till now. So, I got really scared.

Baba didn't stop and kept on firing, "*Khud apne paanv par kulhaadi marte ho aur ab ro rahe ho? Agey kya bhugte ho ge, mujhe dikh raha hai ; fir bhi ab bata hi dalo.*"

I started weeping and told Baba, "Fine, I was wrong…was a fool. So, let's stop it here." Baba came to me, hugged me and said, "*Dil mat chota karo, yeh mera pyaar tha jo pata nhi kahan se nikal aaya.. apne andar jo bhi bacha hai, usse suna hi daalo.*"

Chapter 7

So I told Baba that this is the last and only for you.

I was observing one thing that on one side, she was equipping herself indirectly with papers to stamp herself being my "legal wife" while on the other side, had started spending more time with her family members in Bhopal through phone calls, video calls or visits.

Seeing all this, raised a red flag again and I would always feel that some X factor was playing a role somewhere due to which she wasn't mentally and emotionally with me! She was somewhere else all the time, which I wasn't able to gauge where.

Also, it used to be quite intriguing to me that even after being presented as my "wife" from day one to all sections of society, she still wasn't satisfied. As they say, "When life gives you lemons, squirt someone in the eye." So, I started poking her with a query, "What more do you want? Now, this is your house. So, focus on our relationship here unless you have someone else in Bhopal."

Her smart reply always used to be, "*Mai jitna kar sakti hu kar rahi hu and agar meri life me koi aur hota tou mai aapse shaadi kyu karti?*"

At home too, she had no interest in the dream house I had made. I used to spend so much of my time maintaining my garden along with my *mali* and almost used to make innovative changes on a daily basis. Our garden started winning 1st prizes in the annual rose shows but still, she would hardly spend time there.

She had no interest in my dogs. In fact, when my golden retriever, Angel, was sick seriously, she still went to Bhopal and he expired after 3 days! Food preparation was never her priority. It was always in the hands of maids and she never bothered about my preferences. She was quite fond of eating outside in good restaurants and used to give equal company in drinking at home 3 or 4 times a week. Despite me bringing the best of drinks, her usual remarks used to be, "Chari nhi."

Her intentions raised a red flag when just after few days after my 1st wife's death on 26/5/2021 due to Covid in Delhi, she started openly threatening me, "*Ab to vo chali gayi, ab tou marriage register karwa do.*" This was not only the height of selfishness but also a complete lack of sensitivity. I told her, "I am trying to be a nice person but sometimes, my mouth doesn't cooperate."

I couldn't control my anguish and fired at her, " Have some shame and some patience." To which she equally roared, "*Kya kuch galat demand kar rahi hu, apna haak hi tou mang rahi hu.*"

I shouted within me, '*Once you let motherfuckers slide, they start to think they can ice skate.*'

So my legal team basically got our marriage registered on this random day of 6/6/21 in the Tehsildar, Nakti, District Raipur office on the basis of photographs of the wedding ceremony held earlier!

Even after displaying my bonafide and honesty in the relationship and fulfilling all her wishes, especially after marriage registration, I could sense that she suddenly started putting up walls, keeping me at arm's length, and refusing to get closer to me. I was gradually getting certain that our connection would never move beyond a shallow and superficial level. She had virtually declared me as a "VIP - Very Ignored Person."

But I used to get confused because I had heard that "Life is like a sewer. What you get out of it depends on what you put into it." But here was my life. So, what happened then? Did the sewer get choked?

I could also feel that one voice was gradually pushing me to develop " hatred" for her. But the other voice was guiding me, "Hating people is like burning down your own home to get rid of a rat. So, dear, don't stretch it so far. She is your wife. So, have little patience."

After the end of the 1st wave of Covid, I had brought my both parents with me. My mother had started suffering from Dementia by now. So, taking care of my parents was my first priority. I won't say that she wasn't taking care of them but it was superficial.

The frequency of feuds suddenly started increasing because she was now in a new avatar and started showing new shades. I wasn't prepared for this. That tone she started using with me was as cold as the meat in the freezer. The rare cuddles too would feel cold. She would probably avoid eye contact with me, and her overall vibes weren't too positive. Slowly, every 2 or 3 days, any conversation would turn into an argument and every argument would turn into a week of stonewalling.

All of a sudden, her demand for personal space started soaring high and it started leaving me to wonder, '*How much space in a relationship is normal?*'

But although sacrificing to make a partner happy can be a good thing, it may be trouble if you find yourself constantly sacrificing out of a desire to be the "good" partner and satisfy your partner at the cost of your own happiness. I could see that consistently prioritising her needs above mine was paying a cost to my self-esteem and mental health.

But at the same time, I also started realising, '*Yaar, at this age, I have no desire for drama, conflict or stress. I just want a cosy home, good food on the table, to enjoy a fun-filled life and to be surrounded by good, loving and kind people who make me happy.*'

So, I decided that let myself sacrifice a little more to make my partner happy, which can potentially increase trust and happiness. Thus for long-term collective gain as a couple – to help fulfil my partner's dreams and have a more satisfying relationship – I took a serious call to change myself by deleting "expectations from my wife" from my cerebellum.

But even after sacrificing that much, she never expressed gratitude. Thus, she didn't recognise my sacrifice. I never heard words the "thank you," from her which clearly meant that I was being "taken for granted."

She was very clever in presenting her wishes. For example, "Honey, I was expecting a diamond necklace on my birthday or gold bangles on our marriage anniversary. I know you would gift that, won't you?"

"Darling, it has been almost 6 months since we went on holiday abroad." But now, I realise that it was nothing but passive aggression coming in a sarcastic way, leaving you puzzled about whether you should go ahead or not. But 99% of the time, I went ahead. God only knows why. May be internally, there was either a fear factor of losing her or was it my foolish trust in her?

Then, in the early morning of 26/4/2021, I lost my father due to a sudden silent cardiac arrest while he was in his sleep. I was in a state of shock, sorrow and complete emotional numbness because he was hale and hearty even at the age of 90. We both did all the rituals at Raipur. By now, mom's condition too wasn't improving much. So, my whole focus was on her. Availing 24-hour nurses, trying different treatments including Homeopathic as well as Ayurvedic.

Things were moving normally in our lives, but then a month or two before Holi of 2022, Seema started showing a wish to celebrate Holi at Bhopal. I had heard a lot from her about their "Wild Holi celebrations." So I told her to give me some time to decide. I suddenly remembered that my closest batchmate was in Bhopal. He had broken ties with me since the debacle with my 1st wife. I decided that if I went, then it would be a mission for me to restore ties with him after almost 18 years and what better occasion than Holi?

I landed a day before Holi. On the same evening, I completed my mission and I was so thrilled to have achieved it. It was a highly emotional reunion. On the same night, it was time for celebration. Both her brothers, her sister-in-law and her daughter were there and we all started our drinks along with karaoke. Since all of us were reasonable singers, booze and singing went on.

80% to 90% of the time, my drinking has always been controlled. So, I was in full senses while the rest of the members got heavily drunk. My wife was singing a song, and in the next chair, her younger brother was sitting with his elder brother's daughter in his lap. Suddenly, I noticed that Seema and her younger brother were lip-locked. I was stunned. So, I immediately started shooting a video from my phone. Now, while shooting, I saw again that her younger brother was licking Seema's neck and she was enjoying that and thus, continued her singing.

Baba suddenly rose from his bed and started speaking loudly to himself, "*Hey Prabhu, tune yeh sab dikhane ke liye mujhe ab tak jinda rakha hai? Yeh samaj ko kaunsi bimari lag gyi hai? Mai yeh sab nhi dekh sakta , tu mujhe apne pas bula le.*"

I told Baba that frankly speaking, I too was just not prepared for all this but I got suspicious. I asked myself to have patience and look for any more indicators. Although it seemed disgusting at face value, I wanted to be a little more sure about it.

On the day of Holi and the next day, a few more acts of hers caught my attention and gave me some more authentic indications that there was something definitely fishy between brother and sister.

Highly disturbed, we left Bhopal the next day and landed in Raipur by evening flight. On the same night, after taking a bath, I sat down on my bed, opened the subject of what I saw and asked her to explain to me what was going on.

She started laughing, which surprised me but then, I composed myself and shouted, "You laugh because you think it is a joke. You laugh because you think I am joking?"

Her first response was, "*Aisa kuch hua hi nahi.*"

I retorted saying, "You know bloody well that I don't talk shit. I am stating fucking facts! Deal with them. Since I saw everything from my own naked eyes, don't give me bullshit that it never happened!"

The next day, at night, I again started the subject and asked her, "I am giving you one last opportunity to tell me everything."

She started raising her voice and said that she never imagined that my thinking could be so filthy and that I would raise these dirty allegations on a pious relationship.

I was losing my temper so I asked her, "Don't teach me about piousness. Just explain to me about what I saw!"

This time, she said, "This is all a lie."

I really got infuriated and said, "Yesterday you said *aisa kuch hua nhi.* Today you are saying that it's a lie, which of your statements is true?"

She said, "*Kaisi weird baat kar rahe ho*?"

I responded, "Me, weird? Idiot, I'm limited edition." This really pissed me off and I said, "No, I checked my receipt...I didn't buy any of your bullshit/"

In such scenarios, I either cry or turn into a psychopath. When I'm mad, there is no in-between. So, I gave her 3-4 slaps, which she returned with kicks on my face and stomach. I got up from my bed and went upstairs to my guest bedroom on the 1st floor and locked myself.

This was the beginning of the showdown between the two of us from the 1st week of April 2022. I started remaining in my locked room, having food in my room. She didn't bother to approach me for the next week or so.

A week later, I got a call from her younger brother.

He started in a roaring voice, "*Tumne Seema ko mara? Kyu? Itni himmat kaise ki?*"

I knew that an apple a day keeps anyone away if you throw it hard enough. So, I raised my voice and replied, "First, talk with respect and secondly, if you have been briefed about beating, then you must have been briefed about the reasons too."

He said, "Tum batao."

To which I said, "Why should I? You can ask your sister-in-law who has the video of that night."

He kept on repeating, "*Tum bhejo na, uske paas nhi hai.*"

I said, "I could kill you with kindness, but crushing your ego with sarcasm is more my style."

He responded by saying, "Tumhari sari afsargiri mai utar dunga, jyada hawa me mat udo. Tumhe ab tumhari aukat dikhata hu."

I said, "Your guilt is clear since you are trying to bully me only to hide the real issue," and I banged the phone.

I started spending my mornings and evenings on my terrace looking after my plants, doing yoga 2 times a day, listening to Bhajans, Hindi movie songs and talking on the phone with my friends, but never went downstairs for a minute.

Baba was feeling sleepy. So, I requested him to go to sleep. He said, "After listening to your story, *ab neend kahan se ayegee.. tumne yeh sab jhela kaise aur vo bhi iss Umar me? Tum me sehne ki kafi himmat Prabhu ne de rakhi hai.. mujhe hairani ho rahi hai ki uska pariwar samne nhi aya?*"

I told Baba, "*Aya na. Par jis ghatiya tareeke se aya mai khud hil gaya.*"

Baba then asked me to go to sleep and said, "*Agey kya hua , vo kal puja ke baad jarur sunana.. jara dekhu to sahi yeh kaise log iss duniya me jee rahe hai.*"

I left the hut and it was pretty cold outside but still went to the Ganges. It was a full moon and it's reflection on the mighty river looked awesome.

Chapter 8

The next day, after Pooja, Baba looked very serious. He was getting irritated with Radheji over very petty things. I went to Baba and calmed him down.

He said, "Let's sit near Maa Gange."

Once we were there, he sat on the sand and closed his eyes. I was watching his face which had so much of *TEJ* that it was glowing like the Sun. After about 30 minutes, he opened his eyes and smilingly asked me, "Where were we last night?"

I said "*Baba, hum kuch aur baat karte hai.*"

He said, "*Tum agey kya hua vo batao par mai dekh raha hu ki agey acha tou nhi hua hoga.*"

Theek hai Baba, jo bacha hai usse bhi Sun lo taki mera mann bhi halka ho jaye…

It was in the 2nd week of April, when around 11 AM Seema's brothers and sister-in-law suddenly landed at my place and started knocking at my door.

They said, "Come out. We want to talk to you."

I responded, "I don't want to see your faces. So, you can speak across the door to say whatever you want to say."

Her sister-in-law was doing the majority of talking and started asking, "What's the issue?"

I said, don't try to be innocent. Aren't you aware of it especially after I forwarded the video the very next day?"

So, she asked her brother-in-law to explain what I saw.

He responded loudly, "*Yeh admi pagal ho gaya hai.. yeh andha hai.. iska dimag kharab ho gya hai...iske dimag aur aankho ka ilaj karao.*"

To this my wife added, "*Bhai, inka tou kam hi yahi hai, mera naam kisi na kisi se jodte rehte hai, ab aur koi nhi mila tou aapse jod diya*!"

I always knew that backstabbers specialize in saying the wrong thing at the wrong time to the wrong person. So I declared, "No worries. I am sweet as sugar. Hard as ice. Hurt me once. I'll kill you twice."

I got so furious that I shouted, "Liar. It's okay if you don't like me. Not everyone has perfect taste."

There was complete silence from the other side.

Once she uttered those words, I was just stunned as if the ocean was now full of waves and I couldn't see through the other side of the horizon. I sat down with a thud on my bed and felt the heat of lava just thrown over my body. Gradually, it cooled down and I regained my composure.

Those devils were still standing outside. So, I furiously declared, "I must congratulate all of you for giving an excellent performance and you have left me with no other option but to declare the final result of this stupendous act which is just fuck off from my house and never ever come back since this marriage is OVER."

After my announcement, all went silently downstairs. Before leaving, the elder brother said, "*Kunwar sahab please aisa mat kariye.*" I didn't reply.

The Next morning around 10, the elder brother again knocked on my door and said, "*Kunwar sahab hum ja rahe hai par aisa mat kijiye, yeh humble request hai.*"

I replied, "You didn't come on my invite. So, just get lost and if you didn't like my harsh honesty yesterday, then I too don't like your sugar-coated bullshit either."

Once they left, a thought came into my mind as to whether I overreacted. But soon got an inner response, '*Follow your brain. Your heart is stupid as shit.*'

So, I soon realised that it was just a normal reaction to an abnormal amount of crap! After 2 days, my first legal notice for dissolution of marriage was served on her.

To my surprise, a few days later, her mother landed at my door. I made her come inside my room and locked the room. She started with, "*Jisne uska kanyadaan kiya hai, us se aap rishta jod rahe hai*!"

I replied, "Do you think I am deliberately fabricating this story? If yes, give me one reason why I would do that. Moreover, why you all are not explaining what I saw with my naked eyes?"

Then I explained her shortcomings in detail since 2016 and said where are those commitments which you all gave before I took her back in 2016? She silently left my room.

The next day she again came and started, "*Mai uski saari galtiyo ke liye maafi mangti hu, buss ek baar mere kehne par usse maaf kar De.*"

I told her, "That stage is gone and I won't change my decision."

Around lunch time, I was on the terrace when my maid came running and showed me some small white pieces of grain and said, "Sir, madam *ne yeh cheeze matar paneer jo mai bahar chule pe bana rahi thee, usme dal kar bhag gyi.*" I took those pieces from her and told her to throw that sabji and make fresh daal. I sent those pieces to an expert in *Mana Basti* and he informed me on the phone that it's Jaipatri and being a Saturday, it was clearly a "*Jaadu Tona*" to control you.

It was becoming too much for me to handle it. The next day, around 8 AM, I got an email from her elder brother commanding, "*Neeche jao aur meri mother ka bag check kar lo.*"

I replied in mail, "*Tum log pagal ho gaye ho kya*? Why should I check her bag?"

He again mailed me that because you have labelled her a "Thief!"

Now this, I couldn't digest and replied, "When did I say that? I informed you only about her Jaadu Tona."

After a few minutes, her mother landed at my door and said, "*Neeche aakar mera bag check kar le.*"

I opened the door and said, "*Maaji, hath jodta hu, yeh sab tamasha mat kare.*"

She left and after a few minutes, I got an email with a video attachment wherein my wife was recording a video of her mother packing her bag and purse. She in the video is dictating her mother, "*Ek 2 cheez khol ke dikhao na.*"

After seeing the video, I replied to her brother by email, "Don't try to stand too close to the fire. Plastic melts. And I don't chase, I replace. Remember that."

On the same day, I directed my Advocate to file a petition for "Judicial separation."

After a week or so, I got a call from one of my closest industrialist friends, Gautam, with whom I had been sharing what I was going through. He informed me that he had been invited by local MLA Mr Kanhaya Lal to discuss your matter. In the meeting, my wife's younger brother Sanjeev too was present. On a query about why he was being involved, the MLA told him that his name had been suggested by Bhalla Sahab's wife.

He further informed me that in the meeting, Sanjeev started complaining about me, "*Sir, Bhalla sahab meri behan ko marte hai, us par jhuthe ilzam lagate hai, etc.*"

So, the MLA asked Gautam, "*Yaar yeh Sab to galat hai.*"

To which Gautam informed the MLA, "*Kitne saalo se aap Bhalla sir ko jaante hai tou kya mante hai ki voh aisa kar sakte hai?*" To which he responded, "I have known Bhalla Sir since State formation, one of the most brilliant and dedicated forest officers of the state. He was the most favourite officer of our CM Ajit Jogiji. That's why I wasn't convinced of his story."

Gautam then straight away asked Sanjeev, "Aap batao ki aap kya chahte ho?"

To which he replied, "Peaceful exit."

Gautam then informed the MLA that this is what Bhalla Sir has been asking Seema but she has been refusing.

To this, the MLA responded, "Good then it's," and asked Sanjeev how would he like to proceed.

He responded that he would talk to his family members and organise the meeting along with Gautam to settle the issue once and for all. Gautam intervened to say, "This meeting would only be for peaceful exit as wished by you, nothing else."

Her brother replied, "Obviously."

That meeting never took place and Sanjeev went absconding.

After this brief from Gautam, I called my wife on the terrace in the late evening and said, "Aren't you people ashamed of involving MLA and bringing our domestic feud into the public domain?" More importantly, you tried to use the MLA to threaten me but failed because Gautam was there."

To which she responded, "I am not aware of any of this. Why should I tell Bhai to contact MLA?"

I got so furious that I fired at her, "Oh, darling. Go buy a brain. Since the beginning, you have been a pathological liar! The MLA only informed Gautam that his name was suggested by you to Sanjeev."

She just kept quiet and went downstairs.

CHAPTER 9

A few days later, one late evening, I called her on the phone from my room and fired at her, "I don't have the energy left to pretend to like you now. I hate you for indulging in cheap and cunning acts only to cover and divert attention from your immoral acts. I'm not insulting you but describing you. If you're testing my waters, you better know how to swim."

But can anyone believe that she reciprocated with her venom-oozing tongue and hurled the filthiest of Hindi abuses on me along with open threats, "*Tujhe Saale Nanga kar dungi and jail bhijwa ke chorungi.*"

It was indeed a stunning performance. So, I said, "I love the sound you make when you shut the fuck up. You want to be on my level? Climb, bitch."

While sitting with my Advocate Vinod a few days later to sign papers for Sec -10 Application, Vinod suggested, "Sir, I think she should be asked to leave for a month to give us time to think. I would ask Gautam to talk to her." Gautam called up Seema and gave the suggestion.

She told him "ok" but the very next morning, informed him, "Bhaiya, I won't go and would handle it on my own."

I thought of giving it a try myself, so one night, I messaged her to come to the terrace. I asked her first to keep her phone on the table, and when I checked the phone, it was in recording mode. I was so furious but calmed myself and told her, "The application for Judicial separation has been filed. You better accept Gautam's advice so as to give me some time to think whether you deserve another chance or not."

After that, I told her to leave, but in a jerk picked up her phone and said, "It would remain with me."

Once she left, I checked her phone and was shocked to see 16 recordings of my conversations inside my locked room. On the terrace including my two meetings with her mother inside my locked room.

I was disgusted but I first downloaded these recordings on my phone and returned her phone the next morning. While returning the phone, I told her, "You have no shame for spying on your husband? I know you have been speaking fluent shit only to cover your infidelity! I must say that I may not be perfect but at least I'm not fake. But you are fake. You're just like math and I hate math. I am a nice person. But just don't push the bitch button and just remember one thing that karma would slap you in the face before I do."

After a day or two, she called me to book her tickets for Bhopal. After a few minutes, my agent called me and needed a green signal for her air tickets which I gave. My worker Vikas dropped her at the Airport by a private taxi on 26/4/22.

After she left, almost after 1 month, I came downstairs. I went straight to my mom and sat with her for almost an hour. There were tears in her eyes and she kept on holding my hand so tightly indicating, "Please don't leave me alone." I had already requested Vikas Sen and his wife to come daily around 8 PM and feed Mom for dinner and medicines and finally make her sleep. Also, feed my dog, Mylo, take him out for urination, etc., and then put him to sleep in his room.

After 3 or 4 days, Vikas informed me that my wife had been calling him repeatedly for the last few days but he hadn't responded. But today, there was a call on his wife's phone from an unknown number, and since his wife was busy in the kitchen, he picked up the call and shockingly it was my wife.

She started firing at him, "Why don't you pick up my calls? I know you both are going daily around 8 PM, stay there for 2 hours and also feed Mylo. *Mujhe sab pata hai ki vaha kya ho raha hai.*"

Now this was something which I never expected. I asked him to show me the unknown number and it was just unbelievable when checking through True Caller that it turned out to be registered in Vikas Sen's name. How my wife manage a SIM in Vikas' name in Bhopal is still a mystery but Vikas did tell me that in some connection, my wife had taken his Adhar Card picture a few days before leaving for Bhopal.

Now this was turning more and more mysterious. So, listening to my gut feeling, on the same night, I asked Vikas to check my Bedroom for any hidden cameras. With in an hour, two hidden minuscule cameras were located in the hanging chandelier of my bedroom! I just couldn't digest it. So, I asked Vikas to take the cameras along with the chandelier to a computer shop nearby. He called me from the shop and informed me, "Sir, both cameras are in active mode with the camera as well as voice recording but they are being controlled by a remote access password."

I asked him to bring them back, got the videos made and then asked him to check the whole house for more, but while checking my amplifier lying on my deck outside, he found a button-shaped 2.5 W Lithium battery loosely inserted into the remote of my sound system and it was pretty hot.

I googled it immediately and learnt that this battery was charging those tiny cameras and the battery was getting charged through my sound system.

This was beyond my imagination that while I was upstairs, she hired an expert to fix such a complicated spy system to spy on me and only then left for Bhopal. First, she secretly recorded my 16 phone conversations while she was with me and now this!

I just couldn't bear it anymore so informed all her family members that this is what she has done and attached the videos of spy cameras. All these messages were sent on WhatsApp. After a day or two, I sent an emotional message again to her all family members declaring, "Dear Monsoon, I'm breaking up with you. I think it's time I start seeing other seasons. Summer is hotter than you." I also said clearly that this marriage is now over, I don't want her to be seen near my house and that her entry into my house is banned.

CHAPTER 10

It had been almost 4 days since I gave my last narration to Baba. So, besides my routine dips in the Ganges in the morning and at sunset, I was remaining inside my hut. I didn't want to bore Baba with more of my stuff since I could see that it was mentally disturbing him. So, I got so immersed in writing down each and every detail of my journey that I almost forgot the count of my stay in Ashram. I took a count and learnt that it was my 46th day in the Ashram.

I was going towards my hut after the evening holy dip when Baba called me and said, "*Aa jao kafi dino se Aarti me dikhe nahi*?"

I changed my clothes and joined the aarti. After the aarti, Baba asked me to sit and asked me with a smile, "*Beta, kahan rehte ho*? *Kis cheez me duby ho*?"

I told him, "*Baba aap hi tou rasta dikhaye ho, ab chal ke dekh raha hu. abhi us mod par aya hu jiske agey sirf andhera hai.*"

Baba responded, "*Prabhu Ram ki tum par kirpa hai.. vo khud andhero se bahar nikalne ka rasta dikhayenge. 4 din ke baad anyay par nyay ki jeet ka din bhi aa raha hai… tumhe bhi nyay milega.*"

Then, I understood that after 3 days, it was Dusshera. Dusshera was celebrated on the banks of Ganga with diyas lighting and a long puja worshipping Lord Rama. I bought sweets from the market for distribution. I returned to my hut around 10 PM after meals and sat down to write some points for my notes the next day.

I couldn't sleep that night because the last and darkest phase of my encounter with Seema started unfolding itself...

Chapter 11

One month was coming to an end and I had my gut feeling that Seema would definitely return from Bhopal any day. So, I started keeping my main door locked throughout the day and night. Keys used to be with me and my gut feeling proved right when on 6/6/22, she landed at my house. My maids informed me that Madam was standing at the gate and asking them to open the door. I went up to her. She was just carrying a very small handbag. I politely told her to leave since as already informed, her entry isn't permitted.

She didn't leave and spent the whole night lying outside my main gate. I called up her local cousin who was very close to her to take her away. He gave some vague reasons like he was overloaded with work, etc. I could guess easily that it was a planned move. I asked the maids to give her 2-3 bottles of water for overnight.

I kept wondering why despite my clear message to the entire family, they didn't go to the police in Bhopal itself and lodge a formal complaint since they had my written messages as proof. Why did the family send her alone to Raipur and none of the family members accompanied her to my house? Why didn't she go to the local police station, Mana, Raipur which was just 5 minutes away from my house to complain against me by showing them my messages and take their assistance to enter the house in the first place?

The next day too after again being refused entry by me personally, Around 10:30 AM, she still decided to jump the 10-foot-high gate of the residence and straight away barged inside my house through the kitchen. After landing in our drawing room, they first thing she did was to call her local cousin on speaker phone and said, "*Bhai, agar agle 15 min me meri call nhi ati hai, to tumhe pata hai kya karna hai.*" Then, she went straight upstairs to occupy the lone bedroom there.

I had understood by now that this intrusion had been planned by the family well in advance and the plan was to create confrontation. I took an immediate call to inform the police first, and then, withdrew my maids from doing anything for her. She had full access to the kitchen. The refrigerator was full of all essentials and all desired dry and wet rations.

From the very next day, the first thing she started was to visit my 85-year-old mother who was ailing from Alzheimer's disease on a regular basis. Then, she broke such a heavy lock on the door linking her bedroom to the terrace; she broke the pressure pump plugs twice and the solar fencing main supply line. She openly gave life threats to couple of Vikas and Madhu Sen in front of Mom on their visit at night. I started staying inside my bedroom mostly.

While she was in Bhopal, I had informed her on the phone as well as through WA messages and had sent videos of her baggage (all clothes) being packed in trunks and sent to an unknown destination. Despite that, she landed with no clothes only to create drama and earn sympathy. I noticed after 2 days that she started wearing my clothes lying somewhere in the store and I had no knowledge of them.

By the 2nd week of June, both my ailing mother and I were living like prisoners locked in our own rooms in our own house. My mother's health started deteriorating suddenly. There was fear in her eyes and she was hardly able to walk and speak. I started reporting everything to the SP of Raipur and the local police station but they weren't acting on my complaints.

Although my kids weren't present physically in my house, since I had given them access to all in-house and outhouse cameras, they could see how she was torturing us both. I still remember that on seeing the camera recordings both my sons used to weep like anything and urge me daily, "Papa, please move out of this house. Otherwise, God knows what could happen to Dadi's health and yours."

When I asked my US-based neurosurgeon about the reasons for Mom's sudden health deterioration through video conferencing, my doctor asked, "*Aunty kya ho gaya? Darre kyu hue ho?*"

She fumbled and said, "*Seema mujhe maar degi*!"

My doc asked me, "Who is Seema?"

I told him that she was my wife! The doctor was shocked to hear that and asked me to "Keep Aunty away from Seema."

I placed a sticker outside my mother's room saying, "My wife is restrained to meet my mother as per the doctor's advice."

I also lodged a police complaint and the next day, 2 cops visited us, saw my mother and me in locked rooms, went upstairs to meet my wife and then, met me and informed me, "Your wife has promised not to go near your mother's room." But I still kept Mom in lock and key.

She started suffering from seizures. She could no longer walk without the assistance of maids. She could no longer move her fingers to hold even a spoon. It was really hard watching all of this unfold and not fully understanding what was taking place. I was watching my mother morph into someone I did not know.

In the daytime, maids would bring Mom to my room in a wheelchair, She would spend time with me, and have breakfast, lunch and dinner in my room.

But all of us were so scared about opening Mom's lock and making her sit in the wheelchair. One maid would stand outside my door, and then, in a quick motion, I would open my door and Mom would be brought in. The same process was to be repeated for the return of Mom to her room. This cycle was repeated 3 times a day.

One night, while Vikas and Madhu were feeding dinner in my room, Vikas opened another secret. My wife for the last 2 years had been going almost daily outside our huge house and was sitting on the floor of the servant quarters and used to chat on the phone for hours while I used to be in the afternoon siesta. The next day, I confirmed with my two maids and they accepted this fact.

Anyway, life was a mess and I wasn't aware of what she would do the next hour or day. Living like prisoners in my own house and her roaming like a tigress had started taking a toll on me. But she cleverly and shamelessly continued to unleash mental and physical cruelty on us. But my constant worry was my mom's health. Her paranoid attacks were increasing. She had started dog-whistling to target and terrorise my mother and me. Like psychopathic individuals, she used insidious and diverse forms of dog whistling to covertly manipulate and belittle me. Despite my innumerable police complaints, she still escaped consequences, accountability and judgment from the state and I became a villain when she lodged a false and fabricated FIR against me and almost sent me to jail. Seeing the torturous environment at home, I started thinking of leaving my own property and staying outside so as to save my mother. That's why I started shifting my essential furniture and some cutlery, which was not even a quarter of a mini truck. I asked myself, '*Fine, life is hard but stupid. Why are you making it harder by continuing to stay here? Run.*'

Listening to my gut, I literally ran away from my home on 22/7/22 along with my mother and reached Pune and got her admitted to an Old Age Home, TAPAS.

PART 4

CHAPTER 12

It was around Diwali when I had finished penning down notes on my encounters with the opposite gender until now. While going for the morning walk, I couldn't see Baba around so I asked Kailashaji about Baba's whereabouts. He told me that as usual, Baba left last night for his Samadhi in the forests uphill. I wasn't aware of this practice of Baba. I asked him about his return. He said, "Vo tou nhi pata kyunki Baba apne man ke mauji hai."

But Baba did return on Diwali day and called for me. I told him that I was worried about him. He only asked, "Kahan tak pahunche... zindagi ne tumhe bahut rang dikhaye aur inn isstriyo ne tumhari life me kaafi kala rang bhara hai ; tou abb tum vaha aa gaye ho jahan hazaro prashn tumhare samne honge? Tou jawab dhhondo apne scientific tareeke se jaise pehle dhoond rahe the."

I told him, "Baba, I can only say that I am getting more and more confused."

Baba asked me to follow him to Langar. We had organized a big Langar with food and sweets for around 50 people. There was a Sindhi family from Delhi too who were hardcore devotees of Baba for the last 15 years. They too had brought fruits and sweets.

After the Diwali celebrations were over, I went to Baba's room. He was resting. So, I reluctantly asked him, "Baba, I am unable to sleep because of so much meshing up in my mind. So, can I seek a few clarifications?"

He said, "Why not? Don't hesitate."

Excited like a child, I started, "Baba, please tell me,

1. If the intent behind every act of mine in a pious marital relationship has always been positive, pure, giving; even then should you not expect at least a natural positive response?
2. More importantly, what are you expecting in return? Only love, care, emotional bonding and sensitivity are the pillars of all relationships but marital ones in particular! Is this a huge demand?
3. It's theoretically easy to say, "Don't be selfish and just give without expecting any returns, but is it really feasible? For God's sake, we are Humans; not saints.
4. In our Vedas, a woman has been described as a person of pure love, dedication, and sacrifice in our shastras. So how can she today be selfish, insensitive and deceitful?
5. Also, if one member has gradually become a giver only; then why should he continue to get humiliated day in and day out and lose his self-worth and dignity?
6. Life starts getting tough when you start feeling left out in this life journey and thus, start questioning yourself. Is this what you have earned in 65 years of your life? You start losing confidence in yourself. Why you don't have anyone who belongs to you? Why is there no one who understands you, your emotions, your feelings and your sensitivities?

7. *Your "loved ones" (so-called) have no attachment to you; no heart-to-heart bonding. It all looks so artificial and that breaks you internally every hour.*
8. *Why couldn't I become the priority of my own people whereas, I spent my whole life making others my priority? Life gave me millions of opportunities, but why did it never give me an opportunity or show me a path to walk for myself and my own welfare?*
9. *I always tried my best to give my partners complete freedom, never dominated them, gave them the best of material comforts within my limits, and used to go overboard to "create" Happy Moments for them despite my heavy oOfficial duties and responsibilities. But still, why was the final output misery?*
10. *It's so intriguing to grasp that on one side, I was getting so much respect, love and affection from my uniformed staff but on the other hand kept on getting disrespect, deceit and unfaithfulness from my Own! Why did my loved ones who themselves saw so much respect for their partner inside and outside the house; learn anything from my staff? Why did my staff see or feel me as a father, friend and lately, a well-wisher and Messiah but not my own? Why on one side, I could easily see that there was an act of reciprocation from a third party but on the other side, an act of rejection from your own! Why for one, I was a hero but for another a villain? Why for one "social group" I was a complete man and a good human being but for my own, I was "incomplete" and thus deserved nothing.*
11. *Neither did I break nor did I crumble. But was defeated sometimes by myself, sometimes by fate and most of the time, by my own beloved ones.*

12. *Why did I, being stupid, remain an open book to everyone throughout my life? Because everyone read me completely and then, threw me into a dustbin. Now, what's the point of repenting?*

Whether my spouses entered my life only to cause trauma and so much pain. It looks like a planned revenge. Baba, my brain is just filled with more similar queries but I was seeing that in order to preserve their (spouses) identity, neither did they change their attitude nor lessen their demands. In fact, they started taking me for granted and took advantage of my leniency and the freedom I gave but didn't stop there. Finally, in the end, they shamelessly unleashed their multiple infidelities too!

These deep wounds left me in a pool of blood but they were literally spitting right at my face. They were watching me bleed but had developed so much guts that without a care, they were roaring 'If you have balls, hit us.'

I could clearly see that although we were living under the same roof, for my spouses, I just didn't exist. I was clueless about how to survive such an onslaught. I was losing my mental balance and thus, tried to end my life several times but probably, fate wanted me not to go so easily since the quota of wounds and injuries reserved for me wasn't over still!

In the process, my body too started wilting a little and started developing cracks. Thus, I acquired ailments like diabetes, high bp and more deadly acute sinusitis. Being a sportsman and always a healthy man, I suddenly became diseased.

But I showed courage, brought my sportsmanship into play, boosted my inner resolve and fought it on my own without any support from anywhere to come back in shape."

I think I must have spoken for half an hour non-stop and Baba had for all this time listening quietly.

Baba spoke, "Just remember that you won't always get what you exactly want. But remember this. There are lots of people who will never have what you have right now. So, be happy and contended with whatever happens since whatever is happening is written in your destiny. It's all due to your inner nature."

I replied, "Baba, what's wrong with my nature? My nature is built due to my coded gene pool inherited at the time of birth. My genes only taught me to be humble, not to have any ego, to be contended, to be respectful always, especially to women, to have patience, to be a good humane and sensitive person, to take a majority of my calls from heart and rarely from mind, be assertive when it comes to the truth and exert push only when you lose patience for getting disrespected. So, I think my nature has been quite pure until now.

As a forester, Baba, I have an analogy. I always tried to sow quality seeds of trees and flowers which were genetically pure; but many a time, the soil played the trick with their gene pool and manipulated the genes in such a way that the output was predominantly dry, deciduous and thorny bushes and poisonous weeds.

But, Baba, these wild and toxic weeds still kept on happily spreading all over my forest area and destroying the regeneration of other pure and non-toxic flora. So, I had no other option except to burn these wild weeds. But they were so shameless that they still grew. So finally, I had to manually uproot them to save my Forest from future infestations. But while uprooting them, I got injured and got blisters all over my body which took months and months to heal and left permanent scars. Thus, my body as of today has multiple tattoos of different shapes and sizes and my cerebrum has many blood clots which

I hope would dissolve over the period of time by my mental strength and determination embedded in my genes."

Baba intervened with a huge laugh, kept on laughing and said, "How beautifully you did a fusion of forestry and genetics in explaining your dilemma!" Kailashaji said, "Baba, I am seeing you laughing so much after a long time."

I asked Baba, "You are just listening. Probably, I have bored you."

Baba started laughing again and said, "After a very long time, someone who expresses his inner conflicts so clearly and has such deep thoughts visited the Ashram. Your curiosity is just unbelievable. Go and take rest. We could restart our chat tomorrow."

I took His blessings and went to sleep.

CHAPTER 13

The next day, during our breakfast, Baba posed, "How much faith do you have in fate?"

His query took me by surprise but replied confidently, "None, since words like fate and destiny aren't in my dictionary." Baba smiled and asked me, "Okay. Let's go for a small walk in your forests."

It was around 9 AM when we started our walk and the weather was quite pleasant.

We kept walking silently but after about 15 minutes of walking, I initiated a discussion and asked Baba, "Why and who selected the loved ones in my life? Was it God my karma or my fate? As I try to understand, did I have any role to play in being born to my parents? Who created such circumstances that I had no other option but to allow the entry of only specific spouses in my life?

Baba said, "Okay, just forget about God, karma and fate for the time being and let's focus on your journey with your spouses. So, you tell me that since you only chose them under whatever circumstances, you lived with them. Then where and why did these marriages end in fiasco and brought miseries to you?"

I responded, "Baba, that's clever. You are just trying to pull my leg. But I would definitely tell you that I have tried to analyse where I probably went wrong:

1. *I feel that what I didn't have was wisdom. I wasn't a clever man. I was wrong in my judgements by taking people at face value! Right from the day I joined Civil Services, I had this philosophy that I would trust everyone unless proven otherwise. And once I trusted someone, I would give my 100 % to him or her, but more specifically, I trusted my life partners more than 100%. This philosophy of mine doomed my life and did the maximum damage to my life personally. But just tell me, Baba, why shouldn't one trust his wife, his parents, his kids, and his sisters? How can someone even dream of having doubts about the sincerity and faithfulness of these blood and pious relationships? They have the same blood flowing in their arteries and veins. Same genes. It's fine that you don't want to be kind to your life partner because you don't like him, you perceive him only as an anchor but how can you be deceitful, unfaithful, cruel, and a back stabber to someone who has showered his love, care, respect, sincerity and affection in volumes to you?*

   How can you develop so much guts to injure your loved one so openly? Don't you have fear of God who is watching every act and conduct of yours? On one side, you try to display your faith in God by doing all kinds of pujas, fasts, etc., but at the same time, you indulge in grave misconduct and mischief with the people who gave you a life to live. How can such people be so shameless?

   You are trying to befool the God and have no fear of doing so. Basically, it's clear that these fake pujas are only to seek His blessings to protect you from the bad karma you continue to indulge in. So, you aren't selfish to your own people but also to God. So, in a nutshell, if you have the guts to deceive God, for you, humans are just peanuts. It basically boils down to a battle of truth vs lies.

And unfortunately, throughout my life, despite only speaking the truth, I still lost my battles against lies. This is the biggest tragedy of my life.

2. Baba, I now think that sticking to my Ethos. Not modulating them also has been responsible for a plethora of setbacks in my life. I could gauge bloody well that this ethos would ruin me but I have now understood that my Genes didn't allow me to change. I learnt about genetic and acquired characters in my college life. I knew that acquired characters are basically adaptations to counter adverse conditions. It was my bloody subject but still in real life, I didn't acquire any new character despite being amidst storms throughout my life! Probably my genetic character, or say, my genome was so dominant and powerful that it didn't allow any acquired character to come near me. Another Tragedy of my Life!"

3. I told Baba that I always remained under the impression that I have been running my life on "karma. But frankly speaking, to date, for me, karma only meant good deeds. How and who inculcated this habit in me? I believed that it was inside me, in each DNA of my every cell.

4. Because of my habit of persistently seeking answers from my spouses as to why this or that behaviour. Without getting genuine answers, I had this habit of not keeping quiet or ignoring the other person's behaviour. Was this another major reason for conflicts?

   Whereas, obviously, my life partner always had the habit of "keeping quiet, silently planning and playing her games and would always remain in denial mode of my " why" queries.

I think that probably. I just couldn't develop or inculcate the habit of indifference and ignorance as a part of my behaviour. Thus, without amending myself; I continued to give my best with total sincerity as a husband despite being treated shabbily by my spouses.

5. *If I specifically look into my behavioural pattern in the pious relationships of marriage, then both times with both the partners, I displayed this kind of behaviour that I wanted to be closer to them, not only physically, but also mentally. I displayed in more than clear ways that I always wanted to go a little deeper with them.*
6. *I always wanted to spend quality time through casual or intense conversations. I showed the sensitivity of seeking regular feedback from them by asking them questions about how life is going on, if they having any issues, etc. When you are in such a pious relation, you care for her. You want to help that person. You want that person to grow. You want what's best for them.*
7. *But what turned out to be that in both cases, they didn't want me to come closer to them. They never liked my pushing and my persistence for answers. They were not looking for any kind of lectures, advice or suggestions to improve themselves, to become more mature, more educated, more learned.*
8. *Right from the beginning, my spouses were looking for their own independent space. All the time, they were also keen to look for fun and happiness outside our relationship. And luckily, being a wife of a civil servant, provided them with innumerable opportunities.*
9. *I think, throughout my life, I had become habitual to overanalyse issues whether they were related to my performance as a bureaucrat or as a husband or as a father. But this over-analysis always used to be in 2 areas: one, how to improve my*

performance in each of these roles, and second, to find answers to why my spouses weren't playing their natural roles. Why weren't they listening to my advice to become better women? All this analysis used to be 24/7.

10. *I still remember...long back, one of my closest batchmates had given a very wise piece of advice, "Partner, don't analyse any issue so much that the brain gets paralysed. God has given you life to live and not for post-mortem." But somehow, I never thought it to be a bad habit at all. Yes, even after seeing that the time and energy it was consuming of me with no results, I still didn't drop this habit. Why? Probably, because I must have realised that it would have given an indication of my selfish behaviour.*
11. *The real problem with me has been putting my partner first. So, it was me only who taught them that I COME SECOND."*

Baba intervened and said, "Your narrative of your own shortcomings is well in but what's required is to let your guard down. Let people in. Let people get to know the real you. Allow yourself to fall in love. Allow yourself to fall out of love. Allow yourself to feel, because that's what you were born to do. You, as a human being, were born to feel. You'll probably get hurt multiple times before you find your soulmate, but trust me, it's worth it. Finding your soul mate, the person you're really destined to be with is worth however many heartbreaks you experienced before finding this person. It's clear that you never kept your guard up because it may protect you from getting hurt, but it also eliminates the chance of finding someone who can make you truly happy. You cannot truly be living until you allow yourself to feel the emotions that you are supposed to feel. Allow yourself to feel."

I said, "Baba, but acting or taking calls on feelings has been my hallmark. Also, I always believed in, 'Don't tell me that the sky is the limit when there are footprints on the moon.' But how long could I have tolerated people playing with my feelings as well as obstructing my rise to the moon?

I had put my heart and my soul into my work but lost my mind in the process. Now, that was probably one of my biggest blunders. As they say, 'Don't compromise so much in life that people forget you are a human being.' Now I think that yes, I did compromise like hell. Instead, if I had devoted the same energy and time to myself, I would have probably had that satisfaction that at least, I Lived for myself too.

I have been a romantic person but I probably fell in love much too quickly and that resulted in me getting badly hurt. The problem with love is that you lose control and that is a very vulnerable state to be in. I always wanted to have a beautiful relationship with somebody, but it never seemed to work out.

But, Baba, my strategy too was probably faulty. I was trying my best to live that pious relationship with my soul partner, whereas they were looking to live their life with multiple partners outside our marriage. They bloody well had assessed that this stupid man is caring, blindly trusts them, and since he always remains busy in his job, so firstly, he should be used as an anchor only, and secondly, that they can fulfil their inner wishes to play outside the defined arena.

Thats why, Baba, in the most pious game of marriage, when I was left with no option if my life partner living under the same roof, getting the most luxurious life because of me and still feels incomplete and still has no love, care, feelings and sensitivity towards me and lastly, has enormous desire with no shame to indulge in adultery too, it's better to leave such toxic people from your life and move on.

Baba, both times, I had to make this decision forcibly because continuing to live with such poisonous people doesn't make any sense, especially after giving multiple opportunities to them to mend their ways.

So, who then is to be blamed again? Is it my karma phal? What about their karma phal?

It appears to me that basically, if they had not been married to me, then they would not have had these opportunities to defoliate themselves. So, I feel that the only purpose of them getting married to me, or even jumping for a live-in relationship, was that they knew right from the beginning that this world of a civil servant would only provide them ample opportunities to lead a luxurious life and have real fun in life. The bonus was that here was a human being who was caring and always ready to fulfil their desires and expectations. So, they had nothing to lose. Whereas, I was only expecting little a comfort zone from my life partners, a little care, a little devotion and sensitivity towards me. But unfortunately, I met only selfish life partners who were only looking to get their expectations satisfied me, and mind you, these expectations had no limits.

My partners were those people who would say something but do something else. They're those who look like something but they were actually something else. That's what I couldn't read. Throughout my life, I always looked for opportunities or worked hard to create opportunities only and only to give my partners happiness. These efforts of mine were always bonafide since they were visible physically. But still, in contrast, none of my life partners came forward to provide me with some moments of happiness. In fact, they just didn't care for it. Or they, in fact, indulged in acts deliberately taking advantage of my softness to "snatch happiness from me."

If I look back, then I can say that I couldn't gauge the undercurrents flowing in the minds of my partners because I never ever thought of spying on them. I had complete trust in them. Problems occurred only when their 'behind the curtain' acts came to my notice just by chance. But when they got unearthed, it was too late. They had already crossed the Laxman Rekha and had already covered a long distance on their chosen path.

The first time, despite being torn into pieces with such shocking revelations and acceptances, I still desperately tried to do damage control for the sake of my kids. The second time has been a different ball game because she being a real cunning lady has just not only refused to accept her blunders but has gone beserk to crush me.

So, Baba, in a nutshell, this is what I feel that I lost everywhere because of my own stupidities, the karmas being perceived to date as good deeds was just an illusion and it's clear that basically, I am not entitled to any lady love in my current life."

Baba had a mighty laugh. So I asked him point blank, "Are you making fun of me?"

CHAPTER 14

Baba said, "As narrated by you, if whatever your spouses did to you is true, then as Chanakya wrote, 'Speaking lies, deceit, ruthlessness, greed and impurity are the natural flaws' of every woman. Like the 'beauty' of the cuckoo is in her sweet voice, similarly a woman's beauty is in her 'purity'."

I replied, "I haven't read Chanakya. So, I can't comment."

Baba said, "If 'goodness' too crosses its limits then it becomes evil or harmful. It's clear that you gave too much time to your partners and also, you didn't restrain your goodness towards them and they took advantage of that. A genuine man fails to understand the deceit of a 'kamuk' (sensuous/amorous) woman. She cleverly sows seeds of illusion in him that she loves him only and the man gets trapped in this bait. Man comes alone and goes alone. In this life cycle between the two, he alone has to bear the fruits of paap and punya. Khoobsurti hamesha dil aur jameer me hoti hai, log bina jane usse shakl aur kapdo me dhundte hai. Like a flower has aroma, dry wood has fire, and the human body has both atma and pramatma. A person should use his wisdom to try to know both better."

I replied, "All my advice delivered in the politest way to make amends probably used to fall on deaf ears. It is similar to that of the touch of fragrant winds blowing in sandalwood forest. Bamboos neither can have the same fragrance nor become sandal. I had no other option but to sacrifice them."

Baba said, "Yaad rakho, ghamand ek mansik bimari hai, jiska ilaj sirf kudarat aur vaqt karta hai. I can easily see that these 2 women never ever even tried to enter your heart. So, why are you keeping them in your mind? Anything which is a 'hurdle' in your growth, one should sacrifice it ASAP, however valuable it may be. So, you took the right call."

I said, "Baba, my simple logic is, if there is truthfulness in someone's life, he doesn't need तप*. If a man is pure, why should he go to sacred places to take a bath? If has knowledge, why does he need money? If he has love, what other traits are required?"*

Baba answered, "As Chanakya said, 'Earth is stable because ऑफ़ सत्य*, Sun blesses us with his sunshine because of the power of truth and winds to blow only because of truth. On this planet, everything is stable only because of truth. Since you chose the path of truth most of the time, Prabhu would never allow you to face defeat."*

Me: "Why in the world of believers is the credit of success always given to Gods? Baba, if God blesses those who are meritorious and deserve success, then why didn't he give me success? You mean, I didn't deserve it?"

Baba: "Yes, you made some wrong decisions, but remember, even after Laxman told Lord Rama that this golden deer is basically 'Mareech,' still Prabhu Ram fell to that bait. Why? Because that was the way Prabhu had planned to meet Ravan."

I asked Baba, "You mean to say Lord 'orchestrated' this drama and sacrificed his own wife Sita to kill Ravan? If so, then tomorrow, you would say that I won all my battles because of the blessings of the Lord only? Now the irony is that in sorrows, He won't recognize my merits, won't support me. When I stand tall in my adversities, how can He claim that my courage and determination of mine is because of His blessings? Baba, I can't accept these contradictions. Tell me, can the branches, leaves, and flowers of a tree forget that the life they are getting is from roots which are invisible, ulterior and passive?"

Baba said, "Never."

Me: "Then, how can a woman imagine that the blossoming of her life, fragrance in her life and all the comforts in her life are God's creation? How could these women, despite seeing my care and love, not make an effort to enter my heart? I, as a stupid man, never realised that they are highly selfish and such women are bound to turn into deceitful and cunning women in the future. So, kept on patiently bearing their onslaught."

Baba: "It reminds me again of Chanakya Niti where he says, 'When the ocean gets in catastrophic mood, it breaks all its barriers to spreads havoc on land, but a wise man, even in deepest of crisis, remains within his limits and never breaks dignity' So, again I would say that it's Prabhu Ram who gave you those biggest 'assets' with whom you could defeat your adversaries and they finally lost battles because their powers were without the blessings of God."

Baba, continued in his typical heavy voice, "At this juncture, I can only say three things: one, that as soon as you can say what you think and not what some other person has thought for you, you are on the way to being a remarkable man. Secondly, you tried to nurture these pious relationships with good intent. Lastly, the hardest thing in life is knowing which bridges to cross and which bridges to burn. But you have *used your wisdom beautifully for crossing and burning the bridges. Most importantly, Prabhu also witnessed that and He also recorded what others did to you and either would have punished them by now or would punish them for their karma.*

I shouted, "Baba! Now, this is just unbelievable. Are His recordings all within me? If yes, why can't I hear that recording? When would He punish them? Yes, my 1st wife died 2 years back because of Covid and before her admission to the hospital, she had negligible signs of Covid. But my younger son forced her to get admitted. She never came out alive after 1 month of stay in hospital. I was with my sons all the time on the phone, getting them advice from the US, talking to the highest Officials of MAX Hospital Group and arranging my sons' meetings almost daily with all the doctors attending her. But still, she couldn't be saved. I spent 38 Lacs on her treatment and this was for the lady who not only ruined my life, snatched my kids and hadn't been in touch with me for the last 18 long years. So, Baba, what else have I fallen short of in my Karma? Did Prabhu record it?"

To which, Baba replied, "He would decide, but remember, life changes. You lose love. You lose friends. You lose pieces of yourself that you never imagined would be gone. And then, without you even realizing it, these pieces come back. New love enters. Better friends come along. And a stronger, wiser you is staring back in the mirror. No matter how bad it gets, better days are always waiting, hoping you'll make it there to accept the smiles and joy that they're offering."

Chapter 15

While walking for almost 2 hours, we reached a small jharna. Baba didn't look tired at all but I told him to take rest because as per my habit, I wanted to splash water on my face and drink pretty cold but clean sweet water from the jharna which has always made my mind charged and refreshed.

We restarted walking and I just told Baba that I don't care what is in store for me in days to come – love or friends – but my focus right now is on what I lost and why I lost it.

Baba said, "Beta, you must understand that in Vedanta philosophy, the Creator, Ishvara rules over the world through the law of karma. The various schools of Vedanta hold that karma cannot function independently on its own. Instead, they think that God (Isvara) is the dispenser of the fruit (phala) of karma."

I responded, "Baba! I have seen that nowadays, people visit temples, and donate a lot to seek His blessings as a cure for some worldly problems, for example, disease, financial crisis, psychological problems, etc. But if these are on account of past karma and God does not interfere with the law of karma, how can there be any cure? Moreover, since the law of karma is absolute, even an atheist can achieve positive *karma in his life if he does good deeds. On the other hand, these fake visits to temples, daily pooja and religious rituals wouldn't be of any use if you have bad past karma. Please clarify."*

Baba spoke, "It is true that under all normal circumstances, God does not and will not interfere with the law of Karma. God is the creator of the law-of-karma. Why should he break it? There is an extreme reluctance on His part to interfere in human worldly life to change the karma phala (fruits of past karmas) to resolve problems.

But Baba, As it's said, God is considered omnipotent, omnipresent and omniscient and always protects his devotees. If this is true, how can he protect his disciples if he does not interfere and change the events when necessary? He must interfere in response to their prayers. Otherwise, why should we even believe in a God who is helpless?"

Baba replied, "God will certainly help those who do their actions with vichara (self-enquiry, sustained thinking) and viveka (discrimination). The percentage of that help is determined by the intensity of our prayers against the thickness of their karma phala. When God interferes in the life of a devotee, he does not break the law of karma but just bends it conveniently to defuse the problem for now. One thing is always true – God will never destroy the karma phala. He will just rearrange the events so that the issue appears to be resolved. Eventually, someone has to face the Karma phala at some time or the other."

I smiled and said, "That means He too befools us by just creating an illusion. Okay. That means God too has evolved in Kalyug. Clever and smart."

Baba asked me, "Do you go to any temple regularly? Do you worship any specific God?"

I answered, "No, I don't visit any temple regularly but I have been a believer of God Mata Vaishno Devi throughout my life. Many a time, I have treated nature too as a manifestation of God and thus, with that conviction, dedicated my 37 years of service to serving and protecting trees. But, Baba, Why did you ask me this question? A few minutes before, you talked about Him recording. So, I am curious to know if you have any direct connection with Him."

Baba started smiling and said, "Every human has a soul and that soul is in direct contact with the Creator. It's inside you too."

Now this was a real bouncer. So, I said, "Baba, now you are confusing me. You are shifting gears too fast. Please slow down a bit because all this spiritual talk is just going above my head. I have neither seen Him nor have any idea of what soul is."

Baba said, "Since it's getting late, let's reach the Ashram first and then, we would chat about it after dinner."

We returned to the Ashram, had a dip in the chilly waters of Maa Ganga and finished our dinner. I went for a stroll along Ganga but my mind was on what Baba spoke last. At that moment, Kailashaji came running and said, "Guruji has called you but I am surprised that normally he goes to sleep after half an hour's walk and that too alone."

Baba was waiting. So, he asked me, "Let's walk on the banks of the Ganges." While walking, Baba started, "Before I take you on another important spiritual journey, tell me how would you prove that He doesn't exist?"

I said, "Baba, you always pose questions to me, whereas I am expecting answers from you."

Baba sat down on a rock with his feet in the chilly waters of Ganga and replied, "Unless I have full knowledge about your belief systems, how would I prepare myself to guide you? So, prove that He doesn't exist."

So I told Baba that I could only pose questions. Whether they prove His non-existence or not is for him to judge. "My few queries are:

Q- I ask the Almighty to tell me which mistakes I committed to get this backstabbing from my wives.

As per my knowledge and conviction, I was not committing any mistake and He can certify.

Q- This ethos of mine is responsible for conducting myself in a specific way in marital relationships. Was that a mistake of mine? But He brought me into this world. So, how can they be my mistakes?

Q- Was it a mistake of mine to lead a life with a purpose, to live a life as a man of strong values? Did He insert these values inside me?

Q- Why did He show me the path littered with sharp boulders, and stones and also kept advising me to walk on that path only throughout my life?

Q- Did He only help me to be a good son, to be a good brother, to be a good husband, to be a good father, to be a good professional, to be a man of charity? Did He make me lovable, emotional and sensitive to every human being who crossed me in my journey?

Q- So, if He is responsible for providing me with my Persona or what I AM today, then why did He punish me? People say that God takes care of his devotees. Then, why didn't He take care of me? Why did He still make me suffer?

Q- Why did He make those who had no ethos and were indulging in all kinds of evils succeed in their mission?

Q- If He was inside me, why couldn't He see that in these 43 years, I have remained wounded, bruised, injured, and mind you, internally? In every internal part of my body, whether it was muscles, whether it was bones, whether it was endocrine glands, whether it was blood which was circulating 24 hours in my body, there is pain in each and every internal part of my body. Why hasn't He relieved me of these pains??

Q- He could see that after providing happiness to others first, only then did I wish for happiness for myself and that too on a very minimal scale. But still, why did He keep sending devils to snatch even that minimum-scale happiness? Why did He think that I didn't deserve even that?

Q- Why are those who injured me, who bruised me, and broke the very fabric of the pious relationships being allowed to fearlessly roam without any iota of shame?

Q- Could He not record that I basically have remained a loner despite having thousands of people around me? Nobody even showed a minimum courtesy to ask me, how are you feeling? Are you in good health? Did He ask me and provide words of inner comfort?

Q- He should answer me that even after I tried my best to lead a purposeful life, what was He giving back to me? Only humiliation and suffering. I never ever exploited anyone; never ever exploited anyone's feelings. But still, throughout my life, I kept getting exploited. He didn't stop that!

Q- If He was there and could see that I always was an open book. I never shied away. from disclosing my secrets to my life partners. I wanted my companions to know what I feel but what has it resulted in? It resulted in them knowing me fully...each and every secret of my life, and I knew maybe only 20% or 30% of what they were and what they were planning. My plans and my thoughts were always open so they consumed my openness as an opportunity to prepare their plans. Where was He to guide me to close my book?

Q- Most of the time, I was so engrossed in my career that I probably just didn't bother what my companions were up to. But he never even sent any warning message to me to be watchful.

In the end, I can only say that if He is within me, recording every good and bad deed, it's either I was committing sins which I wasn't aware of and he kept on punching me or if my approach to my life has been pure and pious – which I know it was – then why hasn't He been rewarding me? What is He waiting for? For me to die?"

I stopped and was breathing heavily. So, Baba gave me a glass of water. It was around 3.00 AM. So, I asked, "Baba, I don't know whether I succeeded."

"It's quite late now. So, I will answer you tomorrow," Baba said.

I took his blessings and left for my hut. After my routine hot water bath, I lay on the bed. I was feeling empty in my belly as if all my accumulated fat had gone through a liposuction!

PART 5

Cosmic Analysis

CHAPTER 16

The next day, while I was taking my stroll after yoga, Baba came out of his hut. I touched his feet and he said, "Okay, let's sit in the temple because I feel much closer to the Lord there."

Once seated on his favourite assan, he said, "Ramayan pade ho?"

I said, "No, I haven't read our religious texts like Ramayan or Geeta but I am aware of the stories in them but not much about our Hindu Gods like Lord Rama, Lord Krishna, etc."

Baba said, "*Chalo inn Grantho me bhare gyan ke darshan tumhe mai karata hu aur sabse pehle Shree Bhagwad Gita*, also called the Song of God *se shuru karta hu.*"

What I could grasp from Baba's talk in Hindi is being presented here in a summarised way for the benefit of readers.

Quoting from Draupadi- Duryodhan Conversation:

1. The final outcome of every action is due to two factors: our effort (prayatna) and the deferred results of our past karmas, (adrishta phala). The karma that affects us in this life is called *prārabdha* karma, literally, those karmas which have started to fructify. And those prārabdha karmas bear their fruits according to the laws

of karma. The laws of karma, like all laws of nature, are part of Ishvara's creation.

2. Through these laws, Ishvara ensures that the adrishta phala resulting from every act we commit eventually fructifies in our lives, either later in the present life, or in a future life.
3. Ishvara, as karma phala dātā, the giver of the fruits of actions, is impartial – giving us desirable results for our past good deeds, and undesirable results for our past sinful deeds.
4. We are helpless to the extent that we have no choice over which past karmas will yield their results in the present moment. The fructification of our past karma is metaphorically in Ishvara's hands; not ours.
5. But even though Ishvara establishes the so-called karmic current we encounter each day, we still have the ability to use prayatna, i.e., effort.
6. Even though we have no choice over situations born due to past karmas, we are always free to respond to those situations in any way we choose, using our free will and prayatna.
7. In the same way, we can compensate for the so-called karmic current in our lives by making skilful adjustments in the efforts we make.
8. Karma is not fate! Esoterically, karma refers to the totality of our actions and their concomitant reactions in this and all previous lives, all of which determine our future.

So, I said, "Baba, from what I could understand is that Karma is what you can control and destiny is what you can't control."

Baba said, "Just listen to me very carefully. Karma is that you are aware of what efforts or prayatana, you are supposed to do or you can do. Meaning, you have free will. While destiny is that you aren't aware of good deeds or sins of past karma.

He continued, "Karma is that your genes define your intent to do *satvic* karma while destiny would decide whether they would fructify into success or not.

In Karma, you expect returns in this present life, while destiny decides when to give returns.

So, in karma, the only way is to continue doing prayatan/ efforts to negate your past sins while destiny would take the call whether to accept those efforts.

Baba, after drinking a glass of water, further explained, "The fructification of our past karma is metaphorically in Ishvara's hands, not ours and it's He only who establishes the so-called karmic current we encounter each day. Also, understand that when you are born, based on your past deeds, fate would upfront you every day which you can't control. But actually, these are basically opportunities which God gives you as free will to mitigate your fate with your paryatan to shape your destiny as per your choice.

These choices are being offered by Him to you to apply your free will to decide what you want to be, and what your brand image should be. So, He is giving these opportunities on a daily basis. It's up to you how you convert these opportunities to your advantage by making positive and righteous decisions.

Thus, even with predestined fate, one has the ability to change the final results. I.e, Change your destiny by taking the right calls and decisions with wisdom, with ethos. Now, the final results would be positive or negative and would come immediately or would be deferred. It depends on Him.

Efforts are basically prayatan, not karma which would either give positive or negative results. Both are of two types i.e., drishta and adrishta. Drishta results would come immediately but these results would depend upon your past and present pious and sinful acts. Adrishta results mean that results could be deferred by months, years or maybe be next life.

The negative outcome of your efforts in the current life though are beyond your control but still can only be diluted to some extent by following dharma.

There are unlimited myriad of things that come in pairs. And we cannot just have one side of these dualities. And which is what we want. We want all the best stuff without understanding and accepting that if you accept and embrace one-half of the picture, the other half will follow. You cannot have just one half. You will also have the other side of the coin. So, if you are raised up and honoured you will also fall from that and experience dishonour.

The soul reaps the effects of its own actions. If we cause others to suffer, then the experience of suffering will come to us. If we love and give, we will be loved and given to. Thus, does each soul create its own destiny through thought, feeling and action. Karma is a natural law of the mind, just as gravity is a law of matter.

I intervened and asked Baba, "As I understand, my destiny is shaped by my own actions. Now, where does the soul come into the picture? What is its role? Where is it?"

Baba promptly replied, "It is desire and according to the nature of our desires, we are going to engage in different activities. And what is it that is causing desire? What is shaping our desire? It's the kind of consciousness that we have. This consciousness is the soul."

"So, Baba, what you mean to say is that it becomes very apparent that it is really important to determine your state of consciousness and for that, one needs to learn the dark secrets of the soul."

Baba just nodded.

I jokingly remarked, "Baba, you are probably trying to delete my scientific knowledge and mask it with the smoke of spiritual secrets."

Baba started laughing and kept on for at least half a minute. He said, "Yes, you are right but remember, our Vedas and Puranas are much older than your science. So, just hold yourself till I open more well-settled spiritual theories of Hinduism."

I sheepishly replied, "Ji, Baba." I said, "Baba, I am grateful to you for taking me on this journey. The plethora of knowledge shared by you was something which I hadn't heard of. It would take some time to grasp it fully and then, confront you with my assessments."

Chapter 17

It had started getting chilly in Rishikesh. So, I went to the nearby market and from a Tibetan shop, bought 2 heavy pullovers and a heavy blanket. For the next 2 days, I avoided meeting Baba because I wanted to analyse Baba's preachings my way. The more and more I focussed, the more I was getting confused. Frankly speaking, I wasn't getting convinced about these spiritual theories.

So, after 2 days, probably around mid-December, I met Baba after breakfast. I told him with no disrespect to him and not to his knowledge, "I have analysed what all you shared with me but I have my own take on it." He said, "Good, I knew it… So, let me listen to your take."

I started by saying,

"A. The philosophies like destiny can't be changed, you would have to pay for the sins committed in the previous life and Ishwara would decide when the fruits of your sincere efforts would fructify. Why did He frame this kind of unjustified philosophy? What was the rationale behind framing it? Why didn't He frame a fundamental policy that your efforts in your present life whether good or bad life would end with its fructification in that life only? Why did he frame a theory where predestined karmas whose knowledge isn't with us will keep on passing on or keep on emerging like devils to the next life, then to the next? What was the need to create cycles of such an endless journey?

B. If He is omnipresent, watching us live. Then, let Him judge our prayatan of this life and give results of it in this very life. Moreover, since He is supreme, the results He gives too should provide justice to humankind. If a human has committed sins, then punish him in that life. If he did good deeds in his life, award him with a good life so that at least society gets a clear message about which qualities, values and ethos need to be inculcated to get His blessings and that should be the real reason for worshipping Him. Why should people worship Him in blind faith in a hope that someday, if He desires to be happy, He would deliver the prasad of justice to them?"

C. On one side, He tries to convince you that you have choices – free will – to make decisions but He goes missing when you are using your free will to do good deeds. In fact, He punishes you. While He applauds people who, with their free will, choose to commit sins. So, at the end of the day, He himself is building and sustaining an ecosystem where He gives preference to Bad deeds over Good deeds and since it's His wish and free will that would finally prevail.

D. Moreover where is He? I can't see Him but I have to believe that He is there. Why doesn't He show up, talk to us, interact with us and answer our questions?

E. So, Baba, you need to come forward with really solid evidence that He exists.

F. If God could create the entire universe, why could he not routinely perform unmistakable miracles, like regularly sending angels to kill the people committing sins? Or is it that He feels that there is nothing like sins in this world and it's just a second name of abnormality in human perception? Is it so simple? I can't believe it.

G. As per His philosophies, if everything is predestined, your past sins will punish you in this life whenever they want. Whatever has to happen will happen because it's predestined. Then, what's the point in doing good deeds with values in this life and suffering?

H. What was wrong in my own philosophy throughout my life that nobody should get hurt because of me? That's my dharma and I should make people smile, that's my karma.

I. If He can't see my pure conscience, see my desires and award me accordingly, what's the fun of giving us this present life? This is tantamount to basically making fun of me.

J. Since evil and suffering exist, God must not exist or God may exist, but perhaps, He is a weak god, an incompetent one or even an evil one! I have heard somewhere that there are no arguments in His court. Once the sentence has been passed, there is no bail.

K. Just ignoring these philosophies, if I see what type of consciousness I had throughout my life, I've always felt that I must chase this thing again and again even if I come up with less than satisfactory results. I mean I was chasing an experience and was always hopeful that this was just going to be so perfect. For example, if I fell in love with someone, I tried to live a life with them, and when that thing went to crap, I left that person. But because I had gone through that experience, I felt increasingly conditioned to look again. But again, I failed.

L. So, when what I am due to experience inescapably is going to be there as the result of my past choices, and the result of the choices that I am making at this very juncture in my life would fructify would be decided by God at his convenience, how then could destiny be said to be in my hands?

M. Why I should not think, '*Oh well, I created my own luck. It was all because of my intelligence and my hard work?*' But that also does not mean that this idea – the harder I work, the luckier I get – is also a reality.

N. When I gained maturity, I was given a stair to climb. Let's say it had 20 steps and each step had 2 parts; one was my official career and the other was my marital career. As per my own evaluation, if everything had gone smoothly, I would have been standing at step no 20 because of my ethos, truthfulness and dedication in both careers. I deserved to be there.

But today, unfortunately, I am standing at say step no 16 or 17. From here, when I look down, I see how difficult this climb has been. None of the steps I climbed came smoothly or effortlessly. To climb each step, I had to struggle and face harassment and humiliation in both careers. In both careers, whenever due time came to climb the next step, I was backstabbed and pulled down. I could see that the deserving climb was being pulled down deceitfully and deliberately. Baba, where was God all through this journey? Why did he not show His miracles even once? Forget about miracles, did He not find me worthy of a helping hand even once to pull me to the next step? I fought as a warrior but all alone, pushed myself with all my might every time to climb the next step. More importantly, this derailment every time wasn't for a few days or a few months but varied from 2-3 years to 6-7 long years. Baba, why couldn't your Prabhu even reduce the period of my suffering by realignment of my karma? Baba, just tell me if according to karma, we are responsible for what we are, then what is the role played by God in our life? If He has so many powers, why didn't He remove my sufferings?

So, Baba, I can conclude that wherever I am standing today, although I am not happy and satisfied still I reached there due to my own effort! If I had left everything to Him, I probably would have been standing in the middle of the stairs.

O. These preachings were probably in place just to create a random social order which lacked ethos, had no place for good deeds and people committing sins right in front of you were not only being let free but were being given awards for winning all their battles and leading a luxurious life.

P. Right from my academy days, I believed that I was in full control of my choices and that my actions, in response to what fate offers us, really matter. I always believed that my destiny was not something I could sit by and let it happen to me. I wanted to create or needed to take action on the opportunities I was presented with.

Q. I always believed in these two very important facets of life:

   1. The only person you are destined to become is the person you decide to be.
   2. As William Shakespeare said, 'It is not in the stars to hold our destiny, but in ourselves.' Similarly, in the words of Jack Welch, 'Control your own destiny or someone else will.'

So, Baba, what I could gather from these authors was that it can be hard to think of our destiny as being separate from our fate if we become accustomed to letting it lead our path. A lot of people look at life with a '*que sera sera*' (what will be, will be) attitude, but I thought about it as something I have control over, and that's why I made deliberate actions to create my desired destiny.

Baba, I always tried to remain true to myself and never remained inactive, passive or followed other people's opinions. I always thought that remaining authentic is the best way to determine not just any destiny but the one that's meant for you. I always believed that it's better to believe that I can control my destiny by making deliberate, conscious decisions than just being passive a bystander. This goes back to creating a life for myself that is in line with my authenticity. Thus, I feel, Baba, that with the same attention we use to build our personal brand, we can try to shape our destiny.

I always asked myself where I wanted my life to be in the next five years and then worked backwards. I knew what my value was and what made me tick. I only majorly decided what and who I want to keep in my life, and what has run its course. I never sat back and let someone or something else guide me along, take the wheel and drive towards my own destination...my own destiny. Was anything wrong, Baba, with this kind of attitude?

That's why I have always loved to visit the sea because it has some potent power which makes me think things I like to really think. Sitting on the shore, watching sea waves coming and touching my feet has always mesmerised me. I have concretised many of my life's important decisions in this mode.

I never wanted to be an ordinary person. I wanted to be different. And since I wanted to be different, it was never with any motive of earning some honours or some awards. It was only to basically think out of the box to nurture every relationship and to make my every role become more and more superior, more and more different from the others.

So, Baba, If I wanted to become different, superior and be a role model (God knows for whom), then:

1. Why should I crib that I couldn't join medicine?? I failed because I didn't work hard to clear pre-medical entrance both times! It's my incompetence; as simple as that!
2. I always accepted my parents' commands until they left me because of the gene pool they passed on to me. Then, how can I blame them for the adversities I faced because of their decisions?
3. When I met both my final life partners for the 1st time, my gut feeling in both cases gave me a clear indication that they weren't meant for me. But still, both times, after some time, I changed my decision in a split second. Why? I think it was probably because, at that particular moment in my life, I was frustrated. I was in a state of mind that I had been left out, my time to find a suitable partner was running out and I was left with no choices. This probably shook my confidence and it did hurt my self-worth. Moreover, I misjudged my life partners because I didn't spend enough time to know them. So, even after rejecting them, I went against my intuition and okayed their entry

into my life! So, if you really ask me, I forced that decision on me and thus, only I need to be blamed for the sufferings I got from them.

4. It was my decision to leave my life partners because their toxicity had crossed all limits. But it was my wish, my call, to trust them and love them blindly. I gave them so much freedom and offered such a luxurious life, and if both of them took advantage of that, then they couldn't be blamed. Obviously, I allowed them to reach those toxic limits. I didn't pull the rug earlier. I trusted them beyond the desired limits. So, obviously, I am responsible for that!
5. Who gave a second chance to my second life partner? Me. Despite my parents and close friends suggesting not to go ahead, I still took her back. Then, if she turned out to be cunning, then whose fault it is? Mine!
6. Why did I choose an honest path in bureaucracy? Why didn't I too become a corrupt civil servant? So, if the chosen path was mine, then I have to be ready to face all the bumps on that path too!
7. Once I took a call to move away from toxic partners and if in retaliation they created a nuisance or ruckus, then I should accept it as their natural counter-strategy.
8. Why should I blame other people for disappointing me? I blame myself for expecting way too much.
9. If I look back, I too have committed sins in this life whether intentionally or unintentionally and thus, why should I crib about my miseries? My sins of this life would be upfront to me. How can I even think or wish that their repercussions shouldn't come this way or that way? It's their choice and I have to bear it, surrender to it."

I knew that a flurry of such rational arguments doesn't usually work on religious people. Otherwise, there would be no religious people. So, I told Baba, "Please forgive me for giving my side of thinking. My logic would go against your beliefs and I sincerely apologise for that."

Baba smiled and said, "No need to apologise at all. But you reject God's existence and then draw a conclusion that you alone are responsible for what you have in life needs, in my view, to be seen from another spiritual angle. But do you want to hear it? Whether you get convinced or not at the end is not my concern but I do feel that you must at least have knowledge of the spiritual theories of Hinduism accepted all across the world. This theory, in fact, has helped even the scientific community to get answers to many mysteries of human life on this planet."

Now, my curiosity rose to hear this theory too since it might help me in my introspection. It might help me understand my life's journey a little deeper and finally might refine my perspective to the conclusions I have already drawn.

So, I told Baba, "I am highly obliged that you are taking so many pains to enlighten me fully despite understanding that the scientific brain of mine wouldn't get easily convinced."

Baba smiled, but this time, his smile, his eyes, conveyed a message, 'Just hear me, son. You won't regret it.'

Chapter 18

For the next 2 days, Baba remained busy because there were 2 families of his devotees from Calcutta. Both the families had been Baba's devotees for the last 10 years, and while chatting with them, they disclosed, "What we are today is purely due to Baba's guidance. For the entire family, including kids, He is our God. He has put us on a path where every day, we make only those decisions which would clean and purify our souls before we depart from this world."

These chats made me more curious to hear Baba. So, after 2 days, I was called by Baba to his temple after breakfast. It was probably Christmas time as informed by those 2 Bengali families.

I told Baba what I learnt from his guests about him.

He replied, "I don't do any miracles but I just impart spiritual knowledge to spread love and divinity." Baba then said, "Ok, if you are ready, then let me give you another perspective of our life." I just closed my eyes and started listening to his vibrant voice.

For the benefit of the readers, Baba's preaching in Hindi is being presented after translation in a summarised way.

"Our Vedas and Puranas revealed the laws of karma and reincarnation, which are now two of Hinduism's most central beliefs. They capsulize our ancient religion's view of life, death and immortality. All Hindus know that they take many births and receive the results of their own actions in this and future lives.

As per the Vedas, all beings are souls and thus, spiritual in nature. Although the body is temporary and eventually dies, the soul is eternal.

After death, the soul is reincarnated, taking birth in another physical body or form. Passing from one life to the next, each soul is on a journey of spiritual development facilitated in part by karma, the concept that every thought and action has a corresponding reaction. One experiences the results of both good and bad deeds over a series of lives. The soul is uplifted through every good action performed and degraded with every bad action.

Stuck in this cycle of birth and death, known as samsara, the soul experiences the results of its karma, through which it becomes more aware of how its actions affect the world and others around it. This growth of awareness enables one to become a more selfless and loving being until enough progress has been made to attain moksha, or liberation from samsara, resulting in complete spiritual existence.

Bhagavad Gita too says,

Consciousness cannot be destroyed. It cannot be burnt, fired, shot. All sufferings of happiness or sadness are to this body. Not to the soul. According to the Hindu religion, the human soul is immortal and never dies. After the death of a human, the soul is reborn in a different body through reincarnation. It is the good and the offensive actions (karma) that determine the fate of the soul.

As per the beliefs, our karmas of the present life determine the length and the form of each of our rebirths (*saṃsāra*). To simplify, each of our actions and moral attributes is going to affect what we receive in our next life.

As the bones, flesh, entrails and blood vessels are enclosed by a skin that renders the aspect of men endurable, so the impulses and passions of the soul are enclosed by vanity; it is the skin of the soul. The soul is like a surname in this time and space matrix. It's the ever-loving, abiding, and continuous connection to your auspicious origin. You can't sell it or give it up. It is not possible. The soul is you. The world before your eyes is finite; the universe inside your soul is infinite.

Penetrate deep into the word 'Om.' Gradually, the word will disappear and only the silence will remain. The word is a support. The meaning is within you. Om brings out that meaning which is hidden in your soul.

Atman is divine consciousness. Atman is believed to be the divinity that resides within each individual. While a person may experience negative emotions and actions such as hatred, greed, and violence, Hinduism teaches that all individuals ultimately have the God-self within them.

Conscience is the light of the soul that burns within the chambers of our psychological heart. It raises its voice in protest whenever anything is thought of or done contrary to righteousness. Conscience is a form of truth that has been transferred through our genetic stock in the form of the knowledge of our own acts and feelings as right or wrong.

Conscience is also a great ledger where our offences are booked and registered. It is a terrible witness. It threatens, promises, rewards and punishes, keeping all under its control. If conscience stings once, it is an admonition, if twice, it is a condemnation, and if stings more than twice, only God can help such a person.

While doing an unrighteous act, Cowardice asks, "Is it safe?" Greed asks, "Is there any gain in it?" Vanity asks, "Can I become great?" Lust asks, "Is there pleasure in it?" But conscience only asks, "Is it right?"

The human life form is unique and different from other life forms in the sense that humans are the only species that allow the soul which is an atomic particle of God's consciousness to realize itself.

Our body is just a machine made out of dead matter. The soul is an atomic spark of consciousness. The soul is atomic in size and can be perceived by perfect intelligence. This atomic soul is floating within the heart, and it spreads its influence all over the body.

Our human soul is surrounded by a causal body called Karana Sarira. The causal body stores the imprints of the ideas, thoughts, actions, and accomplishments of the previous lives in different layers. This is the ultimate truth and is responsible for the spiritual journey of every human soul. The soul is an immortal bridge between the body and God and is surrounded by a causal body, which stores the accomplishments of the person.

Souls take multiple births and come in different human bodies for their earthly incarnations. Not only do souls choose their parents, but when we are living at the source as souls, we decide about our next life and that includes future life experiences, life lessons, and the people we will share our lives with. And soul contracts are drawn.

Sometimes, these cosmic contracts are made by mutual agreement between us, the souls, and the great spirit, aka the source. But sometimes, when we have some karmic debts from our past lives, we are given little choice and are sent off to our next life to learn specific lessons required to settle the karmic balance.

These agreements contain all the details of their future earthly incarnations, including specific parents, birth location, time, siblings, and more. Sometimes, it is the Soul that decides the details of the cosmic contract and sometimes, a Higher Power intervenes while the fate of a soul is being decided. Nevertheless, every soul comes to know and has a perfectly good vision of the future life events it is going to experience on earth, even before it enters the womb of the mother.

So, you and your present life are not a random result of gene combinations but everything that you endured, learned, and defied was part of a predetermined plan which you yourself helped to design! First, it is decided what life lessons a soul will experience in their next birth.

You also must know that we meet the same people in our every life! These souls that we encounter in each and every earthly interaction are members of our soul family. Soulmates or soul family members are those who have been very close and important to us in our human lives.

We might have known them as our parents, siblings, teachers, friends or partners. We have been nurtured and enriched by their presence and thus, we choose to meet them every time we come to earth. That being said, they too have to agree to meet us and be a part of our journey.

One has to remember that just because our life is already planned before our birth, it doesn't mean that we do not have any free will. As human beings, we are capable of deciding what's good for our well-being and can decide to move away from any relationship that thwarts us in our quest to live our best life. The world can break your heart but never allow it to wound your soul.

As Baba had been speaking for almost 45 minutes, Radheji brought milk for Baba and tea for me. While sipping my tea, I asked, "Baba, why is the soul inside me? If I have both heart and mind, I can act on my own. There's no need for another entity called soul.

Baba finished his milk, went to the loo and then said, "It takes time for scientific people to digest this kind of theory because they won't accept it without proof. So, just tell me a computer has an operating system. It has all knowledge of what to do and how to do it, but it cannot sense itself. It doesn't have that consciousness.

Similarly, just consider your live body. Can the body parts act on their own? No. They are lifeless without our 5 senses but can senses do all things alone? No. There is something called the mind which tells us how to do the things. The mind is not enough. We also have something called *Manas*, which tells whether we should do it or not; which is good, which is bad. It can sense feelings like anger, love, affection and hatred.

Both *Buddhi* and Manas cannot act on their own. Inside of all these, there is a light which operates all these things.

That light is your soul (Atma). That is you.

The soul always knows what to do to heal itself. The challenge is to silence the mind. Beautiful souls are shaped by ugly experiences.

The real you and I are the souls, not our human hosts. Our souls are immortal and cannot die. When our human hosts die, we just slip back to our real homes in the afterlife. We stay there for varied periods of Introspection, training, learning new things, and preparing for our next life, usually on Earth. We start a new life with our past memories suppressed in order to tackle lessons we haven't learned, or failed learning in our past life, with a fresh perspective. If you have done negative things in your life and caused pain for other people, you must feel their pain and anguish which removes your guilt and allows you to elevate your spirit to higher levels. The main lessons to learn in life are love and compassion.

This is the model of classical philosophy which views man as a rational soul united to a body and views man as a creature made in the image of God. My argument is that human dignity implies a special moral status for human beings and that this special status ultimately requires a belief in the human soul. Scientific materialism denies the soul and thereby, undermines human dignity, but most materialists find they cannot do without the soul and restore it by various strategies. Classical philosophy is more sensible in claiming that human beings have rational souls united to physical bodies. A person finds it hard to feel the essence of the soul in the body due to the hindrance of bodily desires, emotions, and ego."

Baba smiled and said, "Son, Before all, it's necessary to look after the soul. If you want the head and the rest of the body to function correctly, begin to see yourself as a soul with a body rather than a body with a soul. Every soul is special. They're all beautiful. They're all far more significant than anyone on this planet realizes. I think when people are at their best, they're acting in accordance with their soul. The ones who have gone bad don't have bad souls. They've just given up on keeping in touch with them.

You also must know what Our Scriptures say about the soul:

"All living beings are seated as on a machine made of the material energy."

Bhagavad-gita 18.61

"Never was there a time when I did not exist, nor you, nor any of these kings; nor in the future shall any of us cease to be."

Bhagavad-gita 2.12

"That which pervades the entire body is indestructible."

Bhagavad-gita 2.17

A soul has to repay its evil karma in the same life or future lives, there is no escaping the punishment for evil deeds. Similarly, any good deed will bring the soul rewards either in the same life or in future life. Any suffering throughout life is entirely based on one's own doing.

In this Kali Yuga, it is the stage where evil is extremely prominent and the only way to have a pure soul is by becoming a dharmic or righteous person.

The Bhagavad Gita says, "For whatever objects a man thinks of at the final moment, when he leaves the body - that alone does he attain, O son of Kunti, being ever absorbed in the thought thereof." And the last thought of the dying person inevitably reflects his inmost desire.

Baba stopped and drank water from his copper *lota*. He was serious and was staring into my eyes but that stare was of a mother with love in her eyes for her child. He said, "You must remember that the concept of a 'soul' is a religious or philosophical belief and is not considered a scientific analogy for a gene."

I knew Baba was teasing me so I kept quiet for some time and then said, "Baba, the doctrine of soul explained so minutely took me to another level. It has given me an entirely new dimension to my life journey, but at the same time, you also threw me from top to ground because I suddenly feel inferior because as per this spiritual theory, it's me in the form of soul who is responsible for all the tragedies in my life to date. My body is just an empty house taken on rent again by me, the bricks, and the walls of the house are my blocks of genes storing the information of the soul. The genes too would manifest as per the pre-written script whose scriptwriter too is me. Earlier, I was told God is the doer but now, another entity called the soul has been added as an assistant to the main director, God. It's like I can't see God. So, the same applies to the soul. It is in which form? Solid or liquid or a plasma like the Sun?

With a mysterious smile, Baba said, "Son, I can't and would never ever push you to believe in this doctrine. You are the master of your own thoughts, beliefs and mindset. But God's purpose always is not merely to change hearts, but to change minds too. There is no denial of the role of karma (action) in life. The world is not mechanical and your karma is not going to produce the results according to some mathematical formula. So, just spend more time reading more literature on this spiritual doctrine. You would get more insights." Baba got up, smiled, blessed me and left.

On that night, I decided to leave the Ashram the next day. After breakfast, I went to the market to buy a warm shawl for Baba.

Chapter 19

Before my final departure, I went to Baba's hut and asked him, "*Baba, jaane se pehle apki mere bare me jo bhi rai ab tak bani hai vo bata de aur jo bhi salah dena chahte hai vo bhi agar denge tou mai apne aap ko bahut bhagyashali manung.*"

Baba said, "*Chalo, Maa Ganga ke kinare aaj tumhare sath akhiri baar baithte hai.*"

It was around 9 AM when, while sitting on the sand with his feet in flowing Ganga, Baba started, "Beta, just remember that life is just like a closed room whose one window is always open to nature's development. In this process, all scenes of light or darkness; happiness or sorrow; good or bad keep entering this life form's room. Opening or closing the window is definitely in the hands of man but opening and closing the panels of life's window is beyond man's control. It's in the hands of Prabhu. The Quality Of Life can't be raised unless we raise the Texture of our Thoughts and the Depth of Our Understanding. Moreover, the hands of Prabhu have made '*bhagya rekhaye*' of man and you can see that they are never straight."

Baba, with a mysterious smile, further said, "*Zindagi ka sabse bada thappad kisi se ki gayi umeed marti hai. Tumne apni patniyon se jarurat se jyada umeed rakhi .. tum yeh bhul gaye ki iss matlabi duniya ke makhmali rasto par logo ko barbaad karne ke liye, log aksar pyar ka hi sahara lete hai.*

Tum shayad rishto ko sundar banane ke liye kuch jyada hi gehriyo me chale gaye... kya moti talash rahe the?"

I said, "Baba, yes, no doubt that was my goal. But now, when I flick through all the pages of my own soul, I only see that all the lines are only translations of pain."

Baba smiled, "Never be scared of darkness but beware of those who keep you in the dark. Also just remember:

1. *You would never be able to satisfy anyone*
2. *Despite you living for others, nobody would still respect you*
3. *Even if you wish to change someone, you can't because he is getting fruits of his own karma*
4. *Tum dushmano ko apni safalta se maro aur muskarahat se dafan kar dena...*
5. *Sehne wale me sabr hai, tou karne wale ki aukat do takey ki nhi rehti...*
6. *Jo dusro ki rah me andhera karte hai, ujale unhe bhi naseeb me nhi hote...*
7. *Dukh bhogne wala tou agey chal ke sukhi ho sakta hai lekin dukh dene wala kabhi sukhi nhi ho sakta...*

Me: Ji Baba, samajh gya.. mere hisab se mai gunahgar bhi hu tou apna, maine apne siva kisi ko barbad nhi kiya...

Baba then smiled and said, ""Jab bhi mauka mile to phone se ya message se seema ko keh do "ki tumhare hi karam tumse milne ayenge....buss us din hairan mat hona ... """!!

Aur ant me yeh jarur kahunga ki vaqt par bhi chor dene chahiye kuch uljhano ke hal,beshak jawab der se milenge, magar lajwab milenge."

I said, "Baba, I am highly obliged that you not only gave me a place to live but a place in your heart. You are the one who taught me the real meaning of living. I am feeling so jubilant that looking at this flowing mighty Maa Ganga, I feel like I'm reborn. I want to dedicate a song as a farewell gift to You, My Lord if you permit."

"*Arey! Tum mujhe Lord ki Upadhi mat do par tum gaate bhi ho?*

Chalo, apni Iss kala ko bhi jate -2 dikha hi do," Baba smiled.

Feeling so thrilled, looking at the mighty Ganges flowing in front of me; it seemed Maa Ganga was singing, "*Ruk jana nhi tu kahin haar ke, kanton me chal ke milenge saye bahar ke o rahi o rahi.. o rahi o rahi.*"

Baba got up and hugged me tightly. There were tears in his eyes. Emotions were flowing both ways. I touched Baba's feet to take his blessings and just left the place which gave me a new direction in my life.

I then embraced Radheji and Kailashji who started crying at the top of their voice. I too couldn't control myself. It was all so emotional!

Finally, I left for Rishikesh town on foot but stopped at Laxman Jhula to have a view of the Holy Ganges flowing under me. I closed my eyes and prayed, "You don't flow to serve others. It is just your nature to flow, and by being true to your nature, you are serving the whole ecosystem. I request you to bless me to remain true to my nature as a human being so that I could automatically serve humanity." I opened my eyes, bowed before the Holy Ganga and walked towards the taxi stand of Rishikesh.

I located a private phone booth and dialled my younger son's number. His number was coming busy but finally, he picked up. The moment I said, "Betu," he started shouting and crying, "Ekta come, *Papa ka phone hai.. Jaldi aao,*" but kept on crying. "Papa where were you?? Are you ok? How's your health?" My daughter-in-law too joined. She too was weeping like hell. "Dad, *kaise ho*? We have gone mad for the last 5 months."

I said, "I am fine, hale and hearty. So, just calm down. Where are you people?"

My son said, "Where are you?"

I said, "Taxi stand of Rishikesh."

"Papa, just don't move an inch from there. We are in Dehradun and reaching in 1 hour."

I said, "Fine, but please don't drive fast."

My son was still crying and shouting, "Come, Ekta, just move."

I saw a nearby *ghat* which was almost empty, so I sat there next to the flowing Ganga. I was just wondering when I had come, her colour was brownish and she was in a fiery mood, but now, she is so calm and in bluish green colour. Inside, I felt that this immersion for 137 days on the Ganges as well as in the Ashram allowed me to see the world as it actually is, not through a window or screen. It also helped me to overcome some of my fears and gave me greater confidence in my ability to enter into new situations. Staying on the Ganges River was a different kind of education (and life) experience. I can put it that the Holy Ganga stole my head, my heart, my soul. The current pulls my feet downriver. I have become the river and the river has become a part of me. I also understood that a river is such a "complex, beautiful, multifaceted, varied, troubled, and yet, resilient thing that it overwhelms the knowledge or ability of any academic to comprehend it in any holistic sense. It inspires wonder, curiosity and humility. It feels good to say, 'I know the Ganges but of course, I don't. What I know now better is myself and the Holy Ganga has helped. If I have to describe Ganga with one word, I probably would say 'beautiful,' 'bountiful,' or 'a dancer.'

I was in my thoughts when suddenly, I heard my son shouting, "Papa, where are you?"

I shouted, "Here," and both of them came running. My son and daughter-in-law Ekta touched my feet first. I embraced them with tears flowing from my eyes. My son hugged me so tightly and kept on kissing my forehead, face, everywhere. Ekta too was in tears. My son started shouting, "You left us without telling us. You left the phone too at home. Why did you do all this? You left us half dead. Bhai too hasn't slept all these months."

I asked, "How is Ani?"

He immediately dialled Anirudh, "Bhai, *Papa se baat karo.*"

He too started weeping and kept on and on without saying anything and at the end said, "Papa, I am reaching."

We reached home, had a hot water bath and then drank 2 cups of tea prepared by my son. He makes an excellent tea.

The next day, around 7 AM, I was asleep but woke up to the kisses of my elder son, Anirudh. I was surprised. So, I asked him, "How could you?"

My younger son then said, "Papa, Bhai reached Delhi by night flight from Pune and took a cab then to reach here." I could see that Anirudh was trembling, trying to hide his emotions. So, I took him in my embrace and told him, "See, I am fine and right in front of you." Ekta then commented, "Dad, you have gone so weak!"

I said, "Nothing to worry. Now, with you all, I would recover."

Then after 1 cup of tea and another cup of coffee, I gave them every detail of my journey in Ramji Ashram and my bonding with Baba. I told them that staying for such a long period on the banks of the Ganges gave me another perspective to look at this Holy River which could be beneficial for all of you in the future.

So I told my kids," A river teaches us to be ongoing. It also teaches us that we should keep moving forward in our lives without stopping. Rivers that continue for longer duration are those which are mightier. The more depth there is, the more mighty a river is. So, build depth of knowledge and maturity which would lead you to mightiness.

We should not wallow in our past suffering or unpleasant memories. Instead of becoming stuck in the past or worrying about what could or could not have been done, we should move on with our lives focusing on what can and should be done to improve our lives. No one can change the past, but one can work on the present and improve one's life and destiny.

We have to take advantage of favourable circumstances and negotiate our way through problems and difficulties to achieve our goals, knowing when to practice humility and when to assert our strength. One of the best ways to do it is by knowing your natural and inborn strengths, talents and inclinations, and building your life around them with a matching purpose. If you are struggling too much and unable to make desired progress, it may be because you are swimming against the currents of life. It may be a sign that you have to re-evaluate your thinking, plans and actions.

Like a river flowing to the ocean is basically trying to be part of something bigger than itself, we should daily try to be bigger than ourselves, try to stand tall and strong by having high ideals and values and demonstrate the strength of our character as you build your brand and progress in life. Rivers never flow in a straight line - they crisscross the landscape and find the best path to reach their destination. Similarly, you need to be prepared to navigate through life's challenges and stay the course until you reach your goals."

After listening to my thoughts, my kids commented, "Papa, thanks for sharing these vital lessons with us. Papa, you appear to be an altogether different man. Please don't get into the mould of a Baba. You have lived your life like a free bird. So, remain fun please."

I smilingly told them, "Not at all! In fact, I am ready to start my battle against Seema. All of them said in one voice, "Yes, we are with you, Papa."

Then, I surprised them that I had decided to stay for some time in some isolated place in the Himalayan ranges and one of my close friends would help me in locating a place to stay. Ekta felt angry, "That's not fair, Dad. You want to leave us again?"

I told the kids, "Since both Navya and Ekta are shifting to Delhi and you know that I hate Delhi and Anirudh is shifting to Berlin, so in any case, I have to stay alone. So, let me be where I get peace and tranquillity."

So, after a week, I moved myself to a small 1-bedroom house taken on rent in a small village near Sarahan town of Himachal Pradesh. Navya and Ekta came along with me and left after making all the arrangements like ration and a servant, Chand Bahadur, to cook food and clean the house. They also got me a cute Scooty to move around.

PART 6

Ready to fight

CHAPTER 20

When your trust in someone is broken, you will inevitably experience shock, denial, anger, and sadness – feelings that are, in many ways, akin to the mourning process following a death.

When trust is torn by betrayal, disappointment should be released at once. In that way, the bitterness doesn't get time to take root. But as they say, every time your heart is broken, a doorway cracks open to a world full of new beginnings and new opportunities.

Thus, to explore those new beginnings, back in my new serene settlement, I started taking control of the current scenario after being in isolation for almost 5 months. My very first inner call was, '*I don't break; I bounce.*'

The house was located at the tip of a small hillock with a deep valley in front of me.

Luckily, I got Chand Bahadur, a 54-year-old local who agreed to cook my food, wash my clothes and clean the house. He was very disciplined and God-fearing.

Living this life in solitude, I was enjoying it to the hilt. I had learnt to make Dal and sabji from Bahadur on *chullah* and with my learning of Chapati making in Baba's Ashram, I was comfortable even when Bahadur used to be on leave. Pahadi Aloo sabji and pahadi palak sabji were my favourites.

So, my first goal was to get feedback from my sources in Raipur about her current status. I got to know that Seema continues to occupy my property, living alone but the most shocking was the news that besides her younger brother, she has 2 more paramours and all 3 extra-marital flings have been going on much before live-in started with me.

Frankly, this news didn't stir me at all. Even after knowing about my wife's adultery at my back, indulging in cowardly and unethical acts. She and this society expect me to tolerate her roaming fearlessly like a lone tigress in my own house whereas I continue to live in exile.

It was not clear to me why even after leaving her for more than a year, why she continued to occupy my house. Is she still hoping that I would forgive her? I knew that toxic people enjoy torturing others because one, torture reduces people to their most animalistic and barbaric instincts, and secondly, torture is a sign of moral decay and an erosion of the basic human values that define a human being.

One day, while enjoying black coffee on my balcony overlooking the valley, it reminded me that war doesn't end with sunset. But it restarts with sunrise. So, I pressed the War button and shouted, "Finally, my winter fat is gone. Now, have spring rolls."

I also thought, '*Since my wife has tortured me, why should I be ashamed of telling the world that it can also happen!*' So I closed my eyes, first spit on her face and said, "Darling, before you go, I would like you to take this knife out of my back. You'll probably need it. If you didn't want me to tell people that you were a lying piece of trash, then you shouldn't have been a lying piece of trash. Some cause happiness wherever they go; others whenever they go. Pretty simple. I also remembered that sweet talks are manipulative tools. Scorpion's sting as well as bee's sting cause a lot of distress and pain. Both are poisonous and sooner or later, the time comes when you have to betray your own side, plant bags of heroin in pockets, and beat people on the kidneys carefully so that there are no marks.

Now, I had all the desired ammunition but I knew that the strategy this time had to be different from my battle with my first spouse. Earlier, I was a stupid person and went for a direct collision, and sought separation by proving her guilty, but hats off to our legal system, I lost after facing tortures in the corridors of law for 4 long years.

This time, I had only twin objectives, one, to take revenge for my mother from Seema and secondly to prove to society that I was innocent and just get back my lost repute. So, I decided that this time, 'I won't trip over the bitch but walk over her.' So, no direct collisions but all indirect hits through remote.

My legal team started filing cases in the High Court and in a lower court in Raipur with strong and aggressive pieces of evidence to draw conclusions that "here it's my late mother and me who are the real victims of continued acts of Domestic Violence since April 2022 by her and she has been very cleverly and cunningly playing a victim card. She is only trying to exploit loopholes in our feminine-centric laws as well as the mindset of our Hon'ble Courts by clearly misleading them. She thus has proved to be a psychological liar, a fraudster, a big-time manipulator; and an adulterous lady who attaches no value to the desired conduct of partners in the pious relationship of Hindu Marriage. She is literally a criminal openly and shamelessly indulging in acts of DV against her husband. Such women are a real threat to the social fabric of Hindu Society. She and her family's only motive now is extortion of money from me and the rest is all cheap and dirty gimmicks.

I was now aware that I had a long battle ahead but no worries, I was ready to fight it as aggressively as possible to teach this toxic lady a lesson of her life. I took a vow to punish her, to take revenge for my mother's murder.

The results from my legal battles started pouring in and they were encouraging, which instilled a lot of confidence in me.

It was at this time that I decided to convert all my prepared notes in the Ashram into my second memoirs. I started devoting 2 to 3 hours daily seriously to preparing my first draft of the book. This wasn't only a good diversion but also a morale booster.

Since I left Raipur on July 22 I had lost around 14 kg weight, my Hb had gone down from 16.27 to 11.52; my BP remained on the higher side and twice I had attacks of Acute Sinusitis. So, I switched gears and started on a rich protein diet, short walks in the forest near my house, and enhanced my meditation.

One evening, while returning from a small trek, I reached a cliff at around 11,500 feet. I could see the massive valley down below. So, just for fun decided to shout so as to enjoy the echo. God knows how it came into my mind but I just blasted, "Be with a guy who ruins your lipstick. Not your mascara." As expected, my voice came back to me. So, I was thrilled. Kept on repeating the same sentence for 10 minutes until my throat almost choked.

I was spending more and more time preparing the 1st draft of my book. Indian courts consume a lot of time and one should not expect results to come in months but years. So, I told my legal team not to disturb me much since I knew it wasn't a commercial team but an honest and committed team.

It was in mid-February 23 when my younger son gave me the good news of Ekta's pregnancy. I was quite happy but also prayed that, unlike last time, this pregnancy would be successful. The previous abortion was quite painful for both Navya as well as Ekta.

I also started spending time in search of a suitable match for my elder son, Anirudh, who by now had crossed 37. I got in touch with some private marriage bureaus in Punjab, Delhi and Nagpur being run by professional ladies. Offers started coming; many were good but got rejected by Anirudh after talking to them on the phone or through video calls.

But I was really enjoying my stay amidst nature and that too now in the hills. It was indeed a smooth transition from the banks of the Ganges. It was keeping me in high spirits. I was informed by my lawyers that Seema is displaying her frustration in the courts because they are failing to get a court summons served on me because of the lack of my address. The frustration has grown so much that they are not only moving absurd applications, confronting judges but she herself is trying to lead the charge.

It was in August when I took a clear call never to return to Raipur in the future. Both my sons were very happy with my decision. I asked my younger son to put my house DevSthali on sale. So, he placed it on OLX and makkan.com, plus circulated it amongst brokers of Raipur. It was in September when one of the interested parties from Delhi sent their Raipur representative to see the premises. A fun drama unfolded since Seema refused them entry, and asked them never to come near the house. Otherwise, she would complain to the police and lastly, told them that she is the owner of the house and the house is not on sale. On the directions of Navya, the buyer team video-recorded the whole episode.

I was very furious about her behaviour and could read to what limits she could cross in frustration. So, I asked my legal team to look for a solution to this problem. It was during this period when one night after a few drinks, I unblocked Seema on WhatsApp and sent a message, 'How much does she want to give divorce with mutual consent?' She had the audacity to respond, "*Mujhe aapke sath rehna hai , tou sab bhul ke ek nai zindagi shuru karte hai!*" I replied that you are indeed a shameless bitch and blocked her again. A week later, she sent me an email demanding 5.5 crores, all her jewellery and our dog, Mylo. This just stunned me.

My only surviving paternal uncle, retd Principal Secretary from DRDO was in regular touch with me and was really worried about my future. In one of the telephone talks, he said, "Let me try to talk to her family members for a peaceful exit by arranging a meeting at his place in Delhi. I gave him Seema's elder brother Sharad's email address. My Chacha sent him a very well-worded and polite mail but he responded after a month and refused the offer.

My Chacha was quite upset and he said, "Beta, I am convinced that they won't leave you. They will torture you more because you have been trapped by a cunning family. So, just take care of yourself but I don't think that you would get Justice from Indian courts." I replied, "Chacha, no worries. I would handle it. But you, the eldest in my family, are with me. That's more than enough."

By now, my first draft of the book except the last chapter was ready which gave me a sense of exhilaration. The delivery of Ekta was coming nearer and luckily, everything was normal. The foetus' growth too was perfect. So, I enhanced my prayers for Ekta. It was around mid-October when Ekta got admitted for a C-section procedure since at the last moment, the umbilical cord started entangling the neck of the baby. The next day, Ekta delivered a healthy girl baby and made me a proud Dada. I was so so happy that I went to the nearby temple first, distributed sweets to the whole village, lit my rented house with diyas and burnt Diwali anars until 11 PM. I was dying to hold my granddaughter in my arms. Since she was born on the 9th day of *Navratras*. I told Navya, "We are blessed with Mata Rani."

Chapter 21

After 10 days, I went to Delhi by road, and before lifting the baby, I touched her cute pink feet and chanted, "Jai Mata Di. Welcome." Then, I took the baby from Ekta to my arms and kissed her all over. She was sleeping but then, she suddenly woke up and opened her big eyes with a little smile. It brought tears to my eyes. After having our lunch, Ekta joined us after feeding the baby. At that moment, I was telling Navya how frantically Seema was running from pillar to pillar to locate me.

Ekta said, "Dad can I say something?"

I said, "Why not, Beta!"

She said, "Since you have now become a proud Dada, for the sake of your granddaughter, please get out of this mindset of revenge from Seema. You have deleted her from your life for what she did to Dadiji and you. So, let her face her fate."

At that moment, we just froze.

We left Delhi in the early morning hours and our first stop was at a cute little dhaba where my taxi driver Ramesh and I had not one but 2 cups of masala chai with lots of *adrak* and then restarted.

With the cool wind blowing on my face, I told Ramesh not to drive above 80 and just closed my eyes.

What kind of anonymous bullets are being fired by this system where words like hard work, rights, truthfulness and honesty too are getting injured? How long will the white lies of this world will continue to become headlines and the truth will continue to see the faces of dead spectators helplessly?

A time comes in everyone's life when he is standing at a crossroads and he has to choose between 2 paths. One of 'Hope' and the other of 'Revenge' Now, it was my turn to select the right path. I asked myself, '*What would I gain by choosing the path of revenge?*'

You would succeed in settling the score with one wicked and cunning person. But is that what I want? Yes! But why? It reminded me of Baba saying, "Because a cunning individual is more lethal than a snake. Since a snake would attack only in defence this man because of his inherent nature would continually keep on giving you pain. An elephant can be controlled by a small *ankush* a horse by a small tap of the hand but a cunning person should be slaughtered by a sword only since he can't be controlled and, thus has to be destroyed. Another thought that whether my small story can wake up a Kumbhkaran-like system and make a difference. Why not?

Fine, but wouldn't my story in the public domain just be another number in similar stories already floating in the public domain?

My mind was juggling; I was in a dilemma.

Which path should I choose? I remembered Baba's words, "*Jindagi me kuch aisa karo ki Andhiya bhi chalti rahe aur Diya bhi jalta rahe.*"

Thus, I took a conscious call that my first step would be on the path of "Revenge since when the lady of the house abandons modesty and faithfulness, that proves that she has been distracted from her dharma. Then, she becomes a cause of insult to family and this lowers the esteem of the family in the society.

She is a silent predator and thus, has to be destroyed by any means. That's my dharma.

After that, I would walk on the path of 'Hope' where my small story would become more meaningful in the eyes of society. I am confident that in times to come, political leaders, lawmakers and policymakers will be forced to amend their gender-biased mindset as well as gender-biased laws in favour of men.

Then, my story would be the part of that 'change.'

Suddenly, my thoughts were broken by the phone call from Navya.

"Papa, where did you reach? Had breakfast or not?"

"Betu just crossed Rampur and yes, had 2 cups of tea and then, had gone to sleep."

"Papa, you must try *Chole Bhature* at Mid Way coming after another 42 kilometres. You would love it."

"Ok, Beta, *ab bhookh bhi lag rahi hai.*"

"Take care, Papa."

I told Ramesh to stop at MidWay. Chole Bhature was really awesome. I ordered sweet lassi too. After this sumptuous breakfast, we started our last leg of the journey.

As the mighty Himalayas started appearing on the horizon, I felt rejuvenated. But my inner voice asked me, '*Buddy, it seems you are feeling sad.*'

I said, "Yes, the way my younger son so enthusiastically showed me all the paintings, decorative items, artefacts, unique Bastar art pieces, unique tables and chairs which once used to be part of my official house in Raipur; I realised that they were all my prized possessions, mostly gifted to me by my staff, my admirers in MP and in Chattisgarh as a token of their love and respect for me."

Navya kept on repeating, "Papa, look how much care Mom and me took to preserve this treasure of yours".

But I also saw some of my treasures; my premium wrought iron Bastar art side tables plus a few more classy wooden art pieces were rotting on the roof and being used to keep potted plants. I started getting negative vibes.

"Sir, *uthiye apka town aa gaya , apka ghar kahan hai*?" suddenly I heard Ramesh's voice and tapping on my shoulder.

I felt the chill in the air and directed Ramesh to my house. Chand Bahadur was waiting for me. He picked up my suitcase and said, "*Garma garm* chai is ready, sir."

I said, "Good, Ramesh too would have tea."

While sipping tea, I made payments to Ramesh, but while I was sipping my Adrak wali chai, suddenly, a thought scared me. '*Hey, in your absence from your own residence for the last 1 1/2 years, what if Seema too might run away after robbing your DevSthali?*'

CHAPTER 22

Conclusions

My manuscript was getting almost completed but there was no end to all kinds of thoughts flashing every now and then and giving me a dictate, "Hold on! You missed this angle!"

I started getting a little impatient that if this went on, how would I end my introspection? I decided "Fine! another one week for the assimilation of all my thoughts, of all the missed angles, and then, I would close my exercise."

So in the next week, I scanned all my leftover thoughts, analysed them and added relevant thoughts to my manuscript:

1. Why urban women, especially housewives, with no dearth of comfort zones have become so fearless that they can openly declare, 'It's my freedom. I would be left behind if I don't catch up with the current trends?'

   Maybe, it has become a bellwether that these women have become so desperate that they are racing to embrace extramarital flings. One of the backlashes of 'women empowerment' seems to be that the woman who once used to be the foundation of a Hindu family, now cares a fig for the 'strong ethos' of our Hindu family.

This virus is spreading fast but I define these unethical trends as nothing but mental sickness and mental degeneration, which in coming years might tear the very social fabric of our society!

2. My current crisis, for a number of reasons, appears to have parallels to the crisis which I faced with my 1st spouse in the year 2000 onwards. It looks like a 'sequel' made by Balaji Films with the only difference being that the heroine has been changed!

   The basic inner characteristics of both heroines remain the same but this time, Ekta Kapoor probably had a budget crunch so first she didn't pick a beautiful heroine and secondly, made this heroine more deadly, clever and criminal-minded so that the need to have a vamp in the sequel doesn't arise!

   Both times, hell broke loose when the heroine's affairs outside the marriage were uncovered. Both times, the heroine retaliated by first defaming me in public eyes but when they failed; they continued to harass me. Both times, I decided or let's say was forced to escape from my own residence. Both times, while they enjoyed my property, I spent my years as a wanderer in rented shelters.

   The first spouse, except refusing to give me a divorce, left me but neither came back nor disturbed me in my life till her last journey. On the other hand, my 2nd partner is a cunning, cold-blooded criminal who displays audacity today to be with me, making a mockery of the most pious relationship called Marriage."

3. Though in my conversations with Baba, I had argued about the non-existence of God today, I think there is some truth in what Baba used to say. Although you have concluded that you are responsible for success or failures in your life and do take pride in illustrating your good deeds, inherent positive traits, etc. But what I see is that the entry of those who finally came into your life was pre-written, only to punish you for the sins you must have committed in the previous life.

That lends some truth to the Cosmic Theory preached by Baba that He as the Director of this Drama brought me into this world only with a pre-written 'soul script' to purify my sins committed in my previous life and I am just a Daas or "*nimit matr*" executing HIS decisions. I can't say whether it has any truth in it or is just an illusion.

I concluded to let it remain a question mark and closed my exercise. I decided to take a break. So, I went on a trek of roughly 18 km to the nearby Paudiwala Shiv Temple. It wasn't a tough trek and after taking His blessings, returned after 3 days with an overnight stay in a tourist tent.

By now, I was clear that expecting the world to treat you fairly because you are a good person is a little like expecting the bull not to attack you because you are a vegetarian.

So, if I continue to take life too seriously, I will never get out of it alive! Life is too short for regrets. What is life without loss, love without loneliness and ecstasy without pain? You can't have one without the other or you could never appreciate either. One should experience life in all possible ways: good-bad, bitter-sweet, dark-light and summer-winter. One should not be afraid of these dualities. Just as we have two eyes and two feet, duality is part of life. We move in and out of darkness and light all of our lives.

But on many starry nights, I used to wake up and suddenly the thoughts like "Am I alone in this Universe? There is no love on these streets? I have given mine away to a world that didn't want it anyway!"

I remembered Baba's words, "It's the truth of life that we all are born alone and will die alone. So, we need to control our life alone. Maybe at the beginning, it all seems like betrayal and loneliness and you may feel weak. But with time, you will enjoy this newly-found independence. You will find your true self and your true worth. You will enjoy what you will achieve after your struggle, and you will be happy with the decisions you have made."

But one thing was sure that duality did make me more mature and the more mature I became, it helped me to move on and finally made me meet myself. Right now, I'm pleased to be in the light.

First of all, what happens with people who hurt me, is not in my control. I am neither their conscience keeper nor their moral compass. It's not my job to ensure they get punished for being assholes. People play the roles they want to play, and if they choose to play an asshole, that's about it. I cannot do anything about it. But what is in my control is how I choose to let or not let their *dumbfuckery* define my life.

I think, when you bear grudges against people who hurt you, you allow them to take up space in your life. The moment you disassociate from them, saying, '*This person is toxic for me, and I need to stand up for myself now, I need to protect myself now,*' you remove them from your picture. The moment you do that, it's over. Now, whether they die or live or get punished or instead flourish is none of your business. Because it's not your picture. Yes, there is a feeling of vindication, when you see someone who hurt you suffer, and pay for their actions, directly or indirectly, I will not deny that. But that joy never lasts long term. Because Karma is not about them. Karma is about yourself, your soul cleansing and your picture. Karma is going through absolute shit hell, and coming back right up like a king!

There is a famous saying, "If you want to shine, shine like a sun first, burn like a sun." Yes, I always wanted to shine and I really devoted time and energy to shine.

I can easily see what I did throughout my life. I loved my job. I loved every relationship I was in, and I respected every duty of mine, whether in an official capacity or in a personal capacity. But I think the mistake I made was that I started loving the company, not my duty. And as Sir Abdul Kalam says, "You should never love the company because you never know when the company will stop loving you."

On a lighter note, I can use this analogy that life gave me selected cards to play. I played with some and hit a jackpot but with some. I played and it was a disaster. But if I think a little deeper, then I can say that frankly, I never knew how to play with cards. Firstly, I only knew how to play 3 Patti and not any other card game where I had to use my brain to calculate what cards other players on the table could have, etc. I used to play my blind too confidently because I always thought that I had my queen on my side. But it turned out to be my biggest illusion because my queen was never with me but with my opponent because of which, most of the time, I lost badly even on winning cards.

But as they say, life is a difficult game and you can win it only by retaining your birthright to be a person. It's just like there's nothing more beautiful than the way the ocean refuses to stop kissing the shoreline, no matter how many times it's sent away.

So, probably, that's why I hate all those weathermen who tell you that rain is bad weather. There's no such thing as bad weather; just the wrong clothing. So, get yourself a sexy raincoat and live a little.

Before that, I had never thought of it, but now, I feel that probably I was born with wings. Once I gained maturity, I was under no doubt that I was not going to crawl at all. I'm going to use my wings to fly. And that too, when it comes to flying, I never wanted to be an ordinary bird who would take shelter while it's raining. I always tried to fly like the Eagles do, much above the clouds since they have no fear of adversity and have a fearless spirit of a conqueror. Another way of looking at it is that sometimes, we have to be broken down so that we can be rebuilt into what we're actually meant to be.

At this juncture of my life, I also think many a time whether my selection into the most prestigious civil Services was because of God's blessings.

Because one thing is sure. If I had not been a top bureaucrat, I don't think I would have gotten such a respectable status in society, so much of choices, so many opportunities to conserve Nature (another form of God) and finally, gave me a platform to work for the welfare of poverty-stricken forest dwellers as well as deprived kids from the interior most forest areas.

Thus, despite my fate laying "innumerable thorns" in my path, I should not forget that it also gave me a huge bed of roses.

One day while on my routine morning walk, I remembered my conversation with Baba while moving in the forests. I had told Baba, *"Frankly speaking, time taught me a lot but didn't teach on time. That's why today I am a loner."*

Baba's response took me by surprise! He said, "You being left alone proves that you must have made the right decisions in life but do remember that He is with you aur jiske sath voh hai usse kisi aur ki jarurat nhi hai."

"Those who couldn't defeat you by 'running ahead of you' tried to defeat you by 'breaking' you in the life race. So, try to remain silent and focus on winning 'big races' because Duniya ko sunai kam deta hai par dikhta jyada hai."

Frankly, on that day, I felt that I had missed a valuable observation and preaching of Baba.

One night, while remembering the spiritual theory of Baba, I started looking for information on it on the internet. I was shocked that there was a plethora of material on the subject and all lending credibility to the "soul review, soul contract," etc.

To cross-check on this cosmic theory, I just did a rewind of my life events to check on how I made major decisions. It was inner voice, gut feeling.

My gut instinct was something probably I was born with. And this meant that no one had to tell me or guide me. It was just me! Trusting my gut feeling probably made it easier for me to make informed decisions all throughout.

But then, I started wondering whether this instinct or gut feeling was the soul inside me. My vision was now getting clearer. To gain a little more wisdom, I started bisecting each of the major decisions of life minutely and what I learnt is that:

1. This gut instinct always gave me an immediate understanding of something that was happening in my life. I never had to get another opinion or think it over. My gut feeling arose within me like a trusted friend and a gift that I could give to myself.
2. I mostly believed that my gut would help me avoid toxic people and unhealthy relationships.
3. I can now think back to all the times that my instinct told me something, but I chose to ignore it. The little voice inside me seemed to scream, "That's what I'm telling you," as you watched things unravel right before your eyes.
4. Most of the time, I knew what felt right for me and I knew it right from the beginning. Sometimes, I didn't need to search for answers to completely understand the situation. In most instances, my gut feeling gave me a pretty good idea about what to do.
5. As it's said, "Love your guts." For me, it only meant to cherish the inner courage that was within me. It also kept me fully engaged in my own journey and ensured that my inner drive becomes accepted by me. It helped me overcome those inner voices which used to make me afraid of following my passions and become attuned to my own journey.
6. This instinct allowed me to believe in myself above every other thing; made me understand that I can make it and whatever that comes my way is part of my own life journey. The same gut feelings continuously allowed me to follow that path I set for myself. Those things I imagined and decided to do. To see those things as achievable and worthy of my time and efforts.

So I think, I did find some connection between my guts and my soul. As they say, "The soul feels what the mind ignores." Deep in my heart, I know

I am an old soul caged in a young body, that passionately believes in helping people, poetry, literature, romance and all things that make me feel alive in this chaotic world.

Maybe, my soul floating in my guts is guiding me to make all kinds of decisions and remain lively and lovable to every other good soul.

Chapter 23

End

So, I'm still not convinced that my body is just a puppet. To date, whether my soul was carrying me or my body was carrying it, I used my brain and my instincts to make conscious decisions to deliver good deeds to every member of my soul family to the best of my abilities decoded and manifested through my genes. Now, whether it was part of a soul contract or not, I can't say but can say that I have served my soul to date with all humility, purity and devotion by following my duties as a *Kshatriya* should have done. If the purpose of my soul in this life was to gain experience, teach me lessons by punishing me in certain life aspects and improve, then I am optimistic that I have performed well until now and in the process, my guts too gained huge experience in a very short span of time.

One morning, while enjoying my 1st black coffee of the day, sitting on my easy armchair in the small open garden of the hut, I received a voice message from my Batchmate Rakesh settled in Toronto for the last 30 years. We are in regular touch with each other but he rarely sends voice messages. His left side has been paralysed for the last 20-odd years. He finds it difficult to type on the laptop. So, I have been suggesting him to go for voice messages. So, this was a surprise. I listened to the message which said, "Look around you, you will find that sufferings around you are much bigger than yours."

Rakesh has been one friend with whom I discuss everything._

So, I sent a voice message back to Rakesh saying, "It reminds me of famous lines by Gulzar...

सोचता था दर्द की दौलत से

एक मैं ही मालामाल हूँ...

देखा जो गौर से तो

हर कोई रईस निक़ला!"

His text response was, "*vah -2 Pyare, tu tou shayar ban gaya hai...* that's what Meera and I both (Meera is his wife as well as my batchmate) admire about you, you are a Bull Fighter and that's why we love you. *aur pyare yeh bhi yad rakhna, jo har kisi ka ho jaye, uska na hona hi behtar hai...*Meera is sending 3 new stanzas added to the famous evergreen song, '*Lag ja gale.*' Just listen and enjoy your life."

«मुमकिन नहीं है , वक्त की रफ़्तार रोक ले ...

बुझने लगी है ज़िन्दगी, कुछ देर जल तो ले ....

थमने को है यह पॉव भी , कुछ दूर चल तो ले ....

तोफ़ा यह आख़िरी मेरा , अब तो क़बूल ले ...

देने को फिर ,यह आखिरी सौग़ात हो ना हों...

लग जा गले ......ऐ ज़िंदगी ..."

I had tears in my eyes, where the poet magically converted a 'Lover' into 'Life.'

It reminds me of the famous thoughts of Sir Abdul Kalam, "If you want to leave your footprints on the sands of time, do not drag your feet." If I look back, this is what I probably tried to do. I tried to lead a life with a purpose. In every field I was in and every role which I was playing, I tried to make my sincere and honest efforts to leave my footprints. All the time, I was conscious that when I leave this world, at least my footprints should be there on the sand for people to appreciate my sincere efforts, the purity of my soul and my pure consciousness.

That's the reason I never dragged my feet on my selected paths. It was just not there in my behavioural pattern or in my conscious ever to walk by just dragging my feet. I kept on taking long strides to reach my destinations.

I forgave all those people who caused miseries in my life but it doesn't mean that I accept their behaviour or trust them again. It only means that I forgave them for me. So, I can let go and move on with my life.

My instincts never allowed me to cry for any relationship in life. Because I always felt that the ones whom I cried, didn't deserve my tears and the ones who deserved, would never let me cry.

My guts make me feel now that sometimes, we have to be broken down so that we can be rebuilt into what we're actually meant to be. It's also important to remember that everyone has their own unique journey and pace, and it's okay to take things at your own speed.

I would still thank all the people who stabbed me in the back. Because, without them, I would not have known the people who are really there for me. Life is not about who's real to your face, about who's real behind your back. I'm a strong persona and there is a limit to how much I will take. If you lie to me, disrespect me or treat me like I don't matter, I am done.

I always believed, '*Let people misunderstand me. Let them gossip about me. Their opinions aren't my problems.*' I always took a stance to stay kind, committed to love, and free in my authenticity. No matter what my relations do or say, I don't dare doubt my worth or the beauty of my truth.

Even starting my Charitable Foundation, Abhinav in 2016 was a decision made by my gut. One day, while sitting in the office, I got this gut feeling, '*Fine, you didn't get love and care from your own but there are thousands of deprived kids who need love, care and attention and deserve a helping hand. You can and should become their saviour.*' So, my instinct told me, '*Don't wait to be kind. Don't wait for someone else to be kind first. Don't wait for better circumstances or for someone to change, just go.*'

Whatever little I have done to date through my foundation probably did cause a true impact on those neglected, poorest of poor kids. I saw clearly how much they needed that smile I gave them. I also did see how much my support turned someone's entire life around. I have witnessed those emotional moments when someone needed that long hug or deep talk.

It's only because the road I have travelled has not always been an easy one and the path was often full of stones, but I am still here. I know that the only reason I was able to make it this far, the only reason I am still here today, is the fact that my determination and the strength in my belly were walking with me every step of the path.

I have also finally realised that I'm just me. I'm not perfect. I'm me. I've made bad decisions and wrong choices, but I'm me. I've said the wrong things and I've said the right things because I'm me. I don't like everything I've done, but I did it because I'm me. I've loved the wrong people and trusted the wrong people and I'm still me. If I had a chance to start again, I wouldn't change a thing. Why? Because I'm me. There are a lot of good things about me; people just need to look past the imperfections to see what's right.

I am the best, I can be.

I know life is hard. I know how many times I felt like giving up on people and on myself. I know I had good days and bad days but more bad than good or so it seems. I know every day I question myself, '*What is this all for? Am I making the right choices?*' or '*Am I supposed to be here now?*' I know I have more questions than answers and most of the time, I don't even know how to explain them. I know life is hard, but I have to keep going. I have to swim with the waters of my soul, and bloom, no matter how hot the fire is. No matter how many arrows I carry on my back.

But at the end of the day, this is what I am. There is this famous saying, "What defines someone as a 'man' should not be the clothes they wear or how deep their voice is. It should be the content of his character, his strength in the face of overwhelming adversity, and his ability to still love and help others when the world has turned its back on him."

I do believe that I am a warrior. I am a soldier filled with both pain and love. And life, well, life is just another beast I was meant to tame and there is no one better for the job other than me.

I have to understand that people will screw me over. I witnessed things that changed me forever. I lost best friends who I thought would always be there. I cried, I laughed and embarrassed myself. But then, I have found my very own moment, when none of that matters. Where I sat back and realised, '*Crap happens to the people who can handle it. This is who I am and no one can change me, including myself.*'

But as Marie Curie said, "Life is not easy for any of us. but what of that? We must have perseverance and above all, confidence in ourselves. We must believe that we are gifted with something and that this thing, at whatever cost, must be attained."

I always knew that I was born for 'something' and that conviction never allowed to derail me during my 'suffering phases,' because like I never got depressed by the sunset for two reasons: one, I always believed that it has only gone into a sleep mode to rise tomorrow and second, it raises my adrenaline levels since soon, it's going to provide me an opportunity to see another spectacular phenomenon of 'star-filled sky.'

Yes, I took calls sometimes early, sometimes late but I frequently changed gears and took bold calls to lead a life of purity. I always thought, '*Let me be grateful to people who made me happy. They were the charming people who made me happy; they were the charming gardeners who made my soul blossom.*'

A single logic to stop getting hurt for me was believing that nothing is mine. I need to love what I have before life teaches me to love what I lost.

I never watched others doing better than me. I never waited to win but worked to win. I only tried to build my own records every day because I believed that success was a fight between me and myself.

Throughout my life, I have remained a firm believer of a few basic philosophies; First, that "If opportunity doesn't knock, build a door."

Secondly, "I will not follow where the path may lead, but I will go where there is no path, and I will leave a trail." Finally, "Man is not made for defeat. A man can be destroyed but not defeated." Probably that's why, I continued flying like an eagle. So, in the end, I can derive this kind of satisfaction that I did succeed in building my own brand image and I left my own footprints on the sand. I know one thing for sure, whether my spouses or my kids would see my footprints and appreciate them or not but at least there's a large section of people in my life who aren't related to me through blood; but still appreciate and respect my deliverables. Now, that's my real footprint which I have earned!

So, even if I lost the battles, I have that inner satisfaction, the inner conviction that I tried to give the best of me across all the scenarios I faced in my life. I did shine like a sun and I think for anyone, this is the best reward. Since inner satisfaction is the best reward even if people don't recognize that, I don't care but my conscious, my soul is happy, contended and satisfied. Yes, in this present life, I succeeded in living with a purpose.

Obviously, the person I used to be can never come back, because I won't let him. He was naïve. He let his emotions dictate his life.

He was explosive and reckless. He did the best he could though and I'll forever respect him for that. But this new person that I have become came at a price that there are no refunds for unimaginable loss, tragedy and pain. The lessons that I had to learn burned the old me alive. With no guidance or survival guide, the only thing that was left to do was transform. It feels like a whole lifetime has passed, a whole different time and place. But if I look deep enough into my eyes, I can still see him!

Like they say, "Problems will come and go too. We must enjoy the challenges just like we enjoy the waves." Thus, in this current life, I can now say that yes, I faced the challenges and enjoyed beating them. I didn't develop courage by being happy every day, but developed it by surviving difficult times and challenging adversity.

Thanks to those who hurt me; they made me a stronger person.

Thanks to those who loved me, they made my heart bigger. Thanks to those who cared; they made me feel important. Thanks to those who showed concern; they let me know that they care. Thanks to those who left; they showed me that not everything is forever. Thanks to those who stayed; they showed me the true meaning of friendship. Thanks to all those who entered my life; they helped me become the person I am today.

That's why I am still a very, very satisfied man and I'm still going strong in life, trying to make the best of my life, have fun, enjoy my life and enjoy my present moments.

Philosophically, I can say that I followed my dharma since it is the moral duty of an individual's life and dharma dictates that an individual must live their life by established values and virtues, and must do good deeds to strengthen karma, But did following my dharma satisfy my soul? I am not aware. Maybe, it would be judged in the soul conference room after I depart.

This is my Karma that I got my life back, despite hitting rock bottom. That the world seemed to end, except it didn't. That I got closer to where I want to be, in life. That I became the man I always wanted to be. And that I could smile again, laugh again, live again and be me again.

They say karma is a bitch. Thats true. Karma is that bitch who through my soul keeps on coaxing me, "Hey I am not letting you give up. I won't allow you to bow down. You and me, we are going to get through this and we are going to rock."

I think my soul entered my body with a clear predetermined plan to create such life events which would test my resilience. It would hit my consciousness to make righteous decisions and thus become a better soul. I am sure my soul might bring more future life events which will force me to shift and pivot. That's the beauty of the soul guiding you in life. A new day presents a new opportunity for my soul to grow and evolve more.

But I would continue to run for the rest of my years on the rough sands of the shoreline. Even at this age, I still feel young and I'm still aspiring for a better future. My enthusiasm for a happy and fun-filled life is still intact. There is a thrill still in my life. And every day, when I look at myself, my inner voice shouts, '*Buddy, don't look at yourself as a 66-year-old man but an exuberant 50-year stallion.*'

As the saying goes, "What does not kill you only makes you stronger" and "Hardships hurt but they can also bring out the best in us." So, as I view it, "Just as waves in an ocean come and go, we too will. What matters is, did we make a good splash in all these life events?"

Today, I think that my soul has evolved and has made me a man of substance who wrote his own destiny, devoted his life to dharma and whose footprints are there on Mother Earth. A few years down the line, these imprints will be seen on my face, splash all over and would be visible on the sands. Then, people may truly understand me for what I was.

I have only one dream. To become an inspiration for at least my sons. To carry their father's legacy when I am not there.

I am not sure but still think that I would remain in the hearts of many, many people. So, if during my last journey, even one man outside my blood clan thinks and feels that the departed soul was simple, pure and lovable, my soul would be more than happy that this soul lived a life with a purpose and that I would definitely present with pride in the cosmic review and would cherish in the heavens.

The End

"All the adversity I've had in my life, all my troubles and obstacles, have strengthened me… You may not realize it when it happens, but a kick in the teeth may be the best thing in the world for you."

– Walt Disney

www.ingramcontent.com/pod-product-compliance
Lightning Source LLC
LaVergne TN
LVHW091048150826
845673LV00002B/511

* 9 7 9 8 8 9 1 8 6 3 8 7 3 *